PACIFIC
OCEAN

Equator

INDIAN
OCEAN

THE
RIESLING
GRAPE

RIESLING

Stuart Pigott

Series editor: Harry Eyres

VIKING

VIKING

Published by the Penguin Group
Penguin Books Ltd, 27 Wrights Lane, London W8 5TZ, England
Penguin Books USA Inc., 375 Hudson Street, New York, New York 10014, USA
Penguin Books Australia Ltd, Ringwood, Victoria, Australia
Penguin Books Canada Ltd, 2801 John Street, Markham, Ontario, Canada L3R 1B4
Penguin Books (NZ) Ltd, 182–190 Wairau Road, Auckland 10, New Zealand

Penguin Books Ltd, Registered Offices: Harmondsworth, Middlesex, England

First published 1991
10 9 8 7 6 5 4 3 2 1

Filmset in 9/12 point Linotronic Janson Text 55 by Wyvern Typesetting Ltd, Bristol
Printed in Great Britain by Butler & Tanner Ltd, Frome and London

A CIP catalogue record for this book is available from the British Library

ISBN 0-670-82488-7

CONTENTS

MAPS

FOREWORD

When I was seven or eight years old, I had a Ladybird history book about Richard the Lionheart. I have never forgotten the page on which Saladin, the subtle Moor, was pictured slicing a silk scarf with his scimitar while Richard hacked an iron bar in two with his broadsword. It had a double message, both parts of which I think are relevant to the neglected Riesling grape. On the one hand it showed two different approaches to the problem of cutting something in two, both equally effective; but there was also the implication that if it came to a show-down, power would win against subtlety. Light, delicate, appetizing, low in alcohol, wines made from the Riesling grape might seem tailor-made for late-twentieth-century taste. But Riesling has lost out in comparison with Chardonnay, which produces bigger, broader, more powerful wines, often bolstered by the support of new oak.

It is not a question of unfamiliarity: Riesling is without doubt the best-known name among grape varieties, even if it is still too often mispronounced (as Ryezling, when it should be Reezling). Unfortunately, that name conveys to most wine-drinkers something bland, quite sweet and inoffensive. In the English market, Riesling wines are generally identified with the medium-sweet blended German wine called Liebfraumilch, a product which only the German wine authorities associate with the concept of quality. There is the further inconvenience that Riesling's name has been hijacked by certain quite different and inferior varieties, such as so-called Laski Riesling from Hungary and Riesling Italico from Italy. In America, as a delegate to the World Riesling Conference in Seattle in July 1989 explained, Riesling is regarded as a 'user-friendly' sweetish jug wine, suitable for beginners.

Riesling's catastrophic decline in reputation is a sadness to

me and to many other wine writers. The first wine I ever tasted
was a Falkensteiner Hofberg Spätlese 1964, a deliciously grapey
pale-green wine from the Saar valley in West Germany, with a
sweet-sour piquancy which I have found irresistible ever since. I
was only eight years old at the time, and no doubt impression-
able, but the proof of my continuing devotion to Riesling is that
I buy more wine made from that variety than any other. Great
authorities like Hugh Johnson and Jancis Robinson never cease
to proclaim their attachment to the finest estate-bottled German Rieslings, the most aristocratically refined white wines in
the world. The great drinking public, however, resolutely
refuses to go out and buy them.

What is the problem with Riesling? It is not the only grape
from which both sweet and dry wines are made (witness Chenin
Blanc, Sémillon and Sauvignon), but whereas the public is quite
able to accept the co-existence of Sancerre and Sauternes, all
Rieslings seem to be tarred with the sickly brush of Liebfraumilch. The wonderful variety of Riesling wines, from the
steely dry to the exotically rich, is unappreciated. The amazing
ageing capacity of the best Rheingau or Barossa Valley Rieslings is a secret known to very few.

The time is surely ripe for a Riesling revival. Its motor will be
the small, quality-conscious wine estates of the Mosel–Saar–
Ruwer, the Rheinpfalz, the Rheingau and Rheinhessen. No one
knows these estates better than Stuart Pigott. He finds a new,
enthusiastic and dynamic generation of wine-growers in the
German valleys, ready to restore the lustre of their noblest
grape. One may have doubts about the new wave of bone-dry
German Rieslings, all the rage in Germany's gourmet
restaurants (though the best from the Rheinpfalz are world-
class wines), but there are signs of a less fanatical devotion to
dryness at all costs. The important thing, as Stuart so well puts
it, is that the grape's transparency, its ability to mirror the
character of a particular vineyard, is not smothered by excessive
sweetness.

Germany is the motherland of Riesling, but the grape is a
much better traveller than many realize. The full-bodied, dry
Rieslings of Alsace have been building up a steady following:

Stuart reveals that as well as the reliable shippers' blends there is an exciting new breed of single-vineyard wines from the recently established Grands Crus. The Wachau region of Austria is a much less well-known source of great Riesling, but if the wines are as fine as Stuart suggests we must hope that many more reach the merchants' shelves.

In the New World, Riesling is well established in Australia as the most widely planted high-quality white grape. I am a fan of the off-dry, zestful, citrusy Australian Rieslings, so much less fashionable than Aussie Chardonnays, but in some cases quite as good. In California, interestingly, the greatest success has been achieved with sweet dessert wines made from grapes attacked by botrytis (noble rot). These luscious, honeyed, yet refreshing wines may serve to revive interest in the rare, magnificent German Beerenauslesen and Trockenbeerenauslesen on which they are modelled. Perhaps the country with the greatest untapped potential for Riesling is cooler, damper New Zealand, where conditions most closely approximate to those of the Rhine and Mosel valleys.

Riesling may well become the cult grape variety of the 1990s. At the moment it is still misunderstood and undervalued. There is a danger here, because the grape is becoming uneconomic to grow in the steep sites of the Mosel and Nahe valleys, where it achieves some of its greatest triumphs. The advantage to the consumer is that the best Rieslings are still very good value compared to the wines made from varieties like Chardonnay and Cabernet Sauvignon. So, with Stuart Pigott as your inspiring guide, go out and start exploring. I guarantee you will not be disappointed.

Harry Eyres

INTRODUCTION

Riesling: The Vine, Grape, and Wine

Unbeatable quality; indisputably aristocratic. Ludicrously unfashionable.

Jancis Robinson

Riesling has long been acknowledged as the world's finest grape variety for white wines. It is a grape which simultaneously produces the most refreshing and the most complex wines. At their best Riesling wines are both crisp and juicy, flowery and minerally – a miraculous collision of lightness and intensity. However, while fine Riesling wines from the twenty or so countries where the variety is grown on a commercial scale all bear the Riesling hallmarks of vibrant fruitiness and elegance, they appear in a remarkably wide variety of styles. The other noble white-wine grape varieties produce great wines in only one or two styles, but fine Riesling wines cover the entire spectrum of tastes from ultra-light bone-dry whites up to some of the richest dessert wines in the world.

A century ago the finest Riesling wines from the Rhine and Mosel valleys in Germany were the most expensive and renowned wines produced anywhere in the world. Their prices at auction and on British merchants' lists regularly exceeded those of even the finest Bordeaux wines. However, during the last two decades Riesling's reputation as the premier white-wine grape variety has slipped badly. In part, this is undoubtedly due to the current world-wide fashion for wines from the Chardonnay, or Pinot Chardonnay, grape variety. These tend to have a high alcoholic content, and usually both smell and taste of the new oak barrels in which they are made. Riesling wines are quite different in style, invariably tasting crisp and clean however rich and powerful they are.

The more important cause of the declining reputation of Riesling wines is undoubtedly the over-commercialization of Riesling's good name during the last decades. In California, South Africa, Australia, and Eastern Europe wines produced from grape varieties either unrelated, or only distantly related, to true Riesling have long been marketed as 'Riesling'. These have invariably been cheap, sweet wines with none of the elegance or brilliance of genuine Riesling wines. In Germany the names of famous Riesling-producing regions and villages have been used for decades to sell cheap, sweet wines made from inferior grape varieties. No wonder Riesling's good name became tainted with the image of these mass-produced quaffing wines.

During the last few years, however, the world has been slowly waking up to the variety's undoubted nobility. The last five years have seen Riesling storm back into fashion among wine producers in Austria, Germany, Washington State, Oregon, Australia and New Zealand. Demand for Riesling wines has also been increasing in a number of markets round the world, most dramatically in Japan and the Far East.

The official beginning of what Hugh Johnson has called 'an unstoppable Riesling revival' was declared with the staging of the World Riesling Conference in Seattle, Washington State, in July 1989. While events like the Riesling conference are undoubtedly important in rebuilding the reputation of Riesling as one of the greatest of the noble grape varieties, changes in taste and lifestyle look likely to be more important factors in making Hugh Johnson's prediction come true. The demand from restaurateurs round the world for light, elegant white wines, combined with increasing demand for low-alcohol wines as a result of growing health-consciousness, strongly favour the trend to fine Riesling wines.

Riesling's capital as a wine for the dining table is its palate-cleansing acidity, the 'sorbet effect' of its fruity acidity which cuts the fat in rich cream sauces, meats such as pork and duck, and soft cheeses like Camembert and Brie (though Riesling is most at home with fish, shellfish and crustaceans). With careful selection it is possible to find a Riesling wine which will accompany almost any dish that isn't fierily spicy. It is also the fruity acidity of Riesling wines which makes them among the longest-lived wines in the world. In this capacity, they are matched only by the finest wines of Bordeaux.

The extremely low alcoholic, and therefore low calorific, content of Riesling wines is unique among the world's fine white wines. Most dry white wines from noble varieties such as Sauvignon Blanc and Chardonnay have between 12° and 14° of alcohol. Dry Rieslings generally have between 9° and 12°, depending on their region of origin. Top-quality medium-dry and conventional-style German Rieslings can have as little as 7° of alcohol! The great Riesling dessert wines rarely have more than 11°, and often much less, while Sauternes and other dessert wines made in a Sauternes style have 13° to 15°.

For the connoisseur what makes Riesling wines so fascinating is their transparency. In no other white wines can you smell and taste the area from which the wine originated, the weather pattern of the growing season during which the grapes ripened, and the soil on which the vines stood, so clearly as in fine Rieslings. In marked contrast, Chardonnay wines are usually strongly marked by the techniques used by the wine-maker. These techniques can be reproduced in any country where Chardonnay grapes can be adequately ripened. As a result very similar Chardonnay wines can be produced in countries as widely separated as France, California, Australia, and China.

Riesling wines are not easily manipulated into a particular style, but stubbornly tend to reflect where and how they are grown whatever the wine-maker does. They are a bastion of individuality and regional integrity in a wine world where technology, fashion, and modern marketing are tending to standardize the pleasure of wine drinking.

The Character of Riesling Wines

The juice of this, the noblest of all grapes, has concentrated within it all the spice, aroma, and charm which nature is capable of producing.
Kölges, *Handbuch der Deutschen Weincultur und Weinausbildung*, 1837

As any fruit ripens it becomes sweeter and less acidic, turning from green to a warmer hue. Riesling is the latest-ripening white-grape variety in widespread cultivation, and the appearance, smell, and taste of Riesling wines are strongly marked by this characteristic. Riesling grapes almost always have a crisp, tart flavour which is transmitted to the wines made from them. The riper the grapes become, the more this tartness recedes into the background and the more opulently fruity they and the resulting wines taste.

Typically, Riesling wines from the northerly wine-producing regions in the Northern Hemisphere and from the southerly wine-producing regions in the Southern Hemisphere are made from grapes which are barely ripe. They have a pale-greenish straw colour, with a pleasantly tart smell and taste similar to that of fruits on the point of ripening. Without their mouth-watering crisp acidity they would taste rather dull and lifeless. Riesling wines from warmer regions typically have a golden-tinged straw colour, smelling and tasting of fully ripe yellow fruits. They often have a touch of bitterness without which they would be too heavy and bland.

Riesling wines made from extremely ripe grapes, whether vinified dry or with some sweetness, have a peachy smell and taste which is often overlaid by citrus and exotic fruit tones. At this level of ripeness regional character becomes less obvious, though there remains a clear difference between such wines from cooler climates, where this 'over-ripeness' is reached only with great difficulty, and those from warmer climates, where it is normal. The former always retain an elegant piquancy, while those from warmer regions tend to be broad and luscious.

There is, however, a limit to the level of ripeness which Riesling grapes can achieve under normal conditions. Additional richness can be obtained through noble rot or frost – an unlikely-sounding pair, yet it is on them that the great Riesling dessert wines depend for their character.

Noble rot results from the infection of ripe grapes by the *Botrytis cinerea* fungus. Its microscopic mycelium punctures the skin of the grape, allowing the water within to evaporate. The berries shrivel, so concentrating the juice that remains. The botrytis fungus effects a complex series of chemical changes to the skin and juice. These radically alter the appearance, smell, and flavour of the wines produced from the affected grapes. They tend to have a deeper colour, which is often golden or even amber, and both the aroma and taste gain a rich honeyed character. They are also more viscous, and have a concentration of flavour substances as much as two or three times that of a normal Riesling wine.

Since the botrytis fungus rarely infects all the grapes in a vineyard, those affected must be hand-selected during harvest if a dessert-style wine is to be made – an exacting and time-consuming task. If botrytis strikes the grapes when they are unripe, the result is grey rot, or plain 'rot'. If there is heavy rainfall on botrytized Riesling grapes, all is lost. Making botrytized Riesling wines is thus extremely risky and costly. These luscious elixirs are consequently rare and expensive.

Ice wines are made by the other concentration method, freezing, but are no less easy to produce naturally. If ripe grapes are pressed while frozen, part of the water they contain remains in the berries as ice crystals, and the juice they yield will be concentrated. Indeed, it often has a positively syrupy consistency. The more deeply they are frozen the more water turns to ice and the more concentrated the juice and the resulting wine. Ice wines can be made by harvesting naturally frozen grapes, as is done in Germany and Austria, or by artificially freezing the grapes, as is done in many New World wine-producing regions. Ice wines resemble super-concentrated conventional-style sweet Riesling wines, smelling and tasting intensely sweet-sour.

Great ice wines almost burn on the tongue, such is the concentration of sugar, acidity, and extract. They have the highest
acidity content of any commercially available wines. This
makes them virtually immortal. It can also make them very
aggressive in their youth – in his book on dessert wines Stephen
Brook described the great ice wines of the Zilliken estate on the
Saar in Germany as 'lethal weapons'. They need many years, or
even decades, of maturation in the bottle to reach their full
harmony.

The acidity of Riesling wines is an essential part of their
structure, just as the tannins of Cabernet Sauvignon red wines
are an essential part of *their* structure. In both cases the more
commercial wines have rather little structure, and are softer
than their finer relatives. They are best drunk in their youth,
while they retain a good amount of fruit. The top-quality wines
of both varieties can also be impressive while young, having
enough fruit to mask the structure which lies underneath. After
a few years in the bottle they frequently enter a dumb phase
during which they can be quite unattractive. The best wines
emerge from this as they gain 'bottle ripeness' to display their
full subtlety and magnificence.

'Bottle ripeness' is the result of the chemical reactions
between the wine and the oxygen dissolved in it. If the bottle
has a poor cork, wine will flow out and air will enter it, which
accelerates this process. When Riesling wines gain bottle-
ripeness character they take on a mellow, somewhat 'honeyed'
tone. Some can also smell of lanolin, or even 'petrol', depending upon their region of origin. This honeyed character is
quite different from that of botrytis.

Some people don't particularly like Riesling wines when they
reach this stage, preferring the vibrancy of their youth.
However, there is general agreement among experts that fine
Rieslings are best drunk either when still in the first flush of
youth or after maturing for five or more years in the bottle.
Given optimum storage, Riesling wines of top vintages from
the best producers continue to change and develop new
subtleties of aroma and flavour for thirty or more years. The
very best can live perhaps twice or three times this long.

ALCOHOL, SWEETNESS AND ACIDITY: THE BALANCING ACT

The prominent acidity of Riesling wines forms their backbone, but this must be clothed with flesh, with fruit, if the wine is to be harmonious and attractive. In a very good or great vintage nature effects this harmonization process by herself – the warm sunshine of summer and autumn mellows the acidity in the grapes, giving them an intense fruitiness. However, in average or difficult vintages many Riesling wines don't have enough natural fruit and body to balance their often aggressive acidity. (Bottle ripeness softens such wines considerably, but most wine-drinkers are not prepared to wait years before drinking such wines.)

The solutions which Riesling wine-makers have developed to deal with this problem are the addition of sugar to the wine during fermentation to increase its alcohol content, and the manipulation of the fermentation to ensure that the finished wine has some sweetness. In the former case – a process called chaptalization – the extra alcohol helps to obscure the sharp edge of the acidity. In the latter case the unfermented, or residual, sugar left in the bottled wine accentuates its fruitiness and makes it taste fuller.

With the exception of the Wachau in Austria, no Riesling-producing region in the world has failed to adopt either one or both of these techniques; all acknowledge their usefulness in making more harmonious wines, and wine-makers are permitted to use one or both techniques. In several of the most important Riesling-producing regions their more general usefulness as stylistic tools has long been realized. In Alsace, Rieslings are often chaptalized when it isn't strictly necessary, because the producer feels it will result in a better wine. Likewise, in Germany and the New World wine-producing regions the fermentation is often influenced to ensure the finished wine has some residual sugar, because the grower wants to make a wine with a more pronounced fruitiness.

There is no doubt that both these wine-making techniques

can be, and have been, abused. In Alsace many Riesling wines continue to be spoilt by over-chaptalization, while in Germany many Rieslings are still marred by excessive sweetness. Such wines are perfectly drinkable, but lack the elegance which is the hallmark of fine Riesling. On the other hand, in cooler regions modest chaptalization is an invaluable aid in making harmonious dry Riesling wines, and a touch of sweetness makes some of the finest Riesling wines of all.

It is worth noting that alcohol and residual sweetness both act as preservatives, extending the life of the wines. This isn't simply a question of the wine retaining its freshness longer but that the more slowly the process of bottle maturation progresses the finer the result. The most complex Riesling wines are therefore those which have had the greatest concentration of fruit and the best structure in their youth, and have been able to mature in the bottle as long and slowly as possible. As such wines age in bottle the sweetness which might have been rather dominant in their youth slowly recedes, the wine tasting drier with each passing year.

CLASSIC RIESLING AROMAS AND FLAVOURS

In the table of typical aromas below, those of the fruit characteristics of Riesling wines are listed in order of increasing ripeness, those of botrytis and ice wine in order of increasing intensity, and those of bottle age in order of increasing maturity.

UNRIPE	*RIPE*	*OVER-RIPE*
stems	ripe apple	apricot
grass	quince	pineapple
gooseberry	honeysuckle	mango
green apple	orange peel	passion fruit
blackcurrant	peach	guava

BOTRYTIS	*ICE WINE*	*BOTTLE AGE*
almonds/marzipan	rhubarb	lanolin
honey	lemon	honey
dried apricot	fresh pineapple	petrol
mushrooms	baked apple	forest after rain
raisins	marmalade	sherry

Riesling Classifications

Because of the long, slow ripening of Riesling grapes, wines of widely diverging qualities can be harvested by a single producer in a single vintage. In the classic Riesling wine-producing regions of Europe, quality grading systems were developed during the nineteenth and early twentieth centuries to indicate to consumers the style and degree of richness of the Riesling wines produced there. These are now enshrined in the wine laws of Germany, France, and Austria.

The table opposite shows the quality classification systems of the four most famous European Riesling producing regions. Of these only Alsace's, with its division of normal AC Alsace wines from AC Alsace Grand Cru wines, places importance on the wine's place of origin as well as on the level of ripeness in the grapes. Alsace Grand Cru Riesling wines can come only from designated vineyard sites.

In each case the minimum level of ripeness is given in degrees Öchsle and in degrees of potential alcohol. The Öchsle level of grape-juice wine is obtained by measuring its specific gravity (density), as is done with beers, and removing the first one and zero; i.e. a specific gravity of 1080 is equal to 80 degrees Öchsle. Degrees of potential alcohol indicate the alcohol which the wine would have if no sugar was added to the fermenting wine and all the natural sugar in the grape juice was converted into alcohol.

NOTES TO TABLE

1. Wines of the quality grades in italics may be chaptalized.
2. In the Wachau the wines of quality levels marked with asterisks must be fermented dry. In the other Riesling wine-producing regions of Austria the German names for these quality levels are used, and the wines may be either dry, medium dry, or fruity-sweet. As in Germany, Riesling Qualitätswein may be chaptalized in Austria.

	MOSEL–SAAR–RUWER	RHEINGAU	ALSACE	WACHAU
QUALITÄTSWEIN	*50° Öchsle 6.0°*	*57° Öchsle 7.0°*	*AC 65° Öchsle 8.4°*	Steinfeder * 73° Öchsle 9.5°
KABINETT	67° Öchsle 8.6°	73° Öchsle 9.5°	*AC Grand Cru 82° Öchsle 11.0°*	Federspiel * 83° Öchsle 11.3°
SPÄTLESE	76° Öchsle 10.0°	85° Öchsle 11.4°		Smaragd * 94° Öchsle 12.9°
AUSLESE	83° Öchsle 11.2°	85° Öchsle 11.4°	Vendange Tardive 95° Öchsle 13.1°	105° Öchsle 14.7°
BEERENAUSLESE/ EISWEIN	110° Öchsle 15.5°	125° Öchsle 17.7°	Sélection de Grains Nobles 110° Öchsle 15.5°	Beerenauslese and Trockenbeerenauslese wines have never been made from Riesling in the Wachau
TROCKENBEEREN- AUSLESE	150° Öchsle 21.5°	150° Öchsle 21.5°		

The Riesling Vine

GROWTH AND RIPENING

Even at a quick glance, Riesling vines look quite different from those of the other noble white-grape varieties. Most obviously, the leaves are of modest size, are dark green, and have five deeply cut lobes with serrated edges. When the vines are carrying well-developed bunches of grapes they are even more easily recognized. The bunches are medium-sized, seldom much more than 150 mm long and 75 mm across, and are composed of small round berries speckled with tiny brown spots.

Riesling is an extremely robust vine, surviving with ease climatic extremes that would kill almost every other white-wine variety. Owing to its relatively vigorous growth it tends to give quite abundant yields. However, from the grower's point of view, it has the disadvantage of ripening very late. In cool regions it must therefore be late-harvested to reach high quality levels, and can only be planted in the best vineyard sites.

Near the northern limit of viticulture in the Northern Hemisphere the Riesling harvest rarely begins before the beginning of October, and it can extend into the first week of December. Near the southern limit of viticulture, the harvest mostly takes place in April, but it can extend to the end of May. Such late-harvesting carries a high risk, since a period of heavy rain can ruin the crop. Even given such a lengthy ripening period the majority of the crop may reach only 7.5° of potential alcohol. Perhaps Riesling's most remarkable characteristic is that even at such a low analytical level of ripeness it can give pleasant wines.

In these climatic conditions the Riesling vine's vigour can be a problem. If the vines are left unchecked in warm summers with plenty of rain, there is a danger of over-cropping, which results in thin wines. What constitutes a reasonable yield for quality-orientated Riesling producers in cooler climates depends very much on the vintage. Given optimum conditions, 80 hectolitres (8,000 litres) per hectare can be fully ripened, though a yield of two thirds this level will give a noticeably higher quality. Given less than optimum conditions, the lower the yield the better the wine.

In warmer regions Riesling can be harvested earlier, but the more rapid ripening there tends to make for wines with less aroma, elegance, and finesse. Here a big problem is that the hot ripening conditions result in grapes with thick skins. The skins, pips, and stems of grapes all contain bitter-tasting tannins. The thicker the grape's skin the more tannins the resulting wine will tend to contain. While a modest amount of tannins can give the wine more body and make it taste bigger, too much tannin makes it taste heavy and coarse. The challenge to the producer in a warm climate is not to extract too much tannin when pressing the grapes. This is a tough task in the Barossa Valley of South Australia, for example, where the skin of the Riesling grapes can be up to seven times as thick as in Germany's Rheingau region!

SOIL AND MICRO-CLIMATE

Of all the white-wine grapes Riesling is most sensitive to the soil on which it is grown, and in the classical Riesling-producing regions it is not unusual to find growers who can identify the vineyard from which wines originated simply from a wine's aroma. The right soil is important for the vine, both to help the ripening of the grapes and to develop the full complexity of aroma and flavour which its wines are capable of.

A stony or sandy soil warms more quickly than a deep clay one, and a stony soil holds the heat of the day through the night more effectively than a loamy one. In vineyards with sandy or stony soils, growth and flowering begin earlier and the grapes ripen more completely, giving wines with a fine natural harmony. If the roots of Riesling vines sit in water through the summer and autumn because of a deep water-retentive soil, the wines they give will be full-bodied, but with a very firm acidity. On the other hand vines on too dry a soil may suffer from drought, resulting in wines which are rather flat and lifeless.

The mineral composition of the vineyard's soil also has an influence on the aroma and fruit character of Riesling wines. The most obvious example of this is the piquant minerally bouquet of Rieslings from the grey slate soil of the Mosel–Saar–Ruwer's vineyards. However, there are numerous other examples, such as the aromatic peachiness of Riesling wines from vineyards with a red sandstone soil, and the pineappley fruit of those from vineyards with a weathered granite soil.

Micro-climate, that is the climatic conditions specific to a single vineyard, is important in determining the character of all wines. Riesling is perhaps the most sensitive of the noble white-wine varieties to micro-climatic factors. The most important of these for wine quality and character are the vineyard's exposure to the sun and the degree to which it is sheltered from the wind. Different degrees of inclination and exposure can enormously influence the amount of solar radiation a vineyard receives. For example, a 30 per cent slope facing due south receives fully double the solar radiation of a 30 per cent slope facing due north!

TRUE AND FALSE SYNONYMS

Thanks to the ever-wider distribution of Riesling round the world during the last decades, a long list of Riesling synonyms has developed. The numerous attempts by producers of other wines to cash in on Riesling's good name has created an even longer list of false synonyms. This is a position which is counterproductive, since it leads to much unnecessary confusion and in many cases to consumers being misled.

Wines produced from the true Riesling ought to be labelled simply 'Riesling' rather than under one of the correct synonyms, and this designation ought to be banned for all wines which are not from the true Riesling. In addition, varietal names which include the word Riesling, such as Laski Riesling, should be banned, since these varieties are in no way related to the true Riesling. The EEC, and the organizations which regulate the marketing of wines in the other major wine

markets, should act along these lines to protect the consumer
and the interests of producers of wines from the true Riesling
vine.

The following catalogue of true and false synonyms lists by
country of origin all the synonyms which can be found on the
labels of commercially marketed wines. The most important in
each group are printed in capitals. Underneath each false
synonym the true identity of the vine variety is given.

TRUE SYNONYM	FALSE SYNONYM	COUNTRY
KLINGELBERGER	SCHWARZRIESLING (Pinot Meunier)	West Germany
RHEINRIESLING	WELSCHRIESLING (Italian 'Riesling')	Austria
Petit Rhin	Johannisberger (Silvaner)	Switzerland
RIESLING RENANO	RIESLING ITALICO (Italian 'Riesling')	Italy
Rajinski Rizling/ Rizling Rajinski Renski Rizling	LASKI RIESLING (Italian 'Riesling')	Yugoslavia
Rajnai Rizling	PECS RIESLING (Italian 'Riesling')	Hungary
	OLASZ RIESLING (Italian 'Riesling')	
	BALATONI RIESLING (Italian 'Riesling')	
Rezlink Reszlink rynsky		Czechoslovakia

TRUE SYNONYM	FALSE SYNONYM	COUNTRY
Rizling		Bulgaria
Riesling du Rhin	Banat Riesling (Zackelweiss)	Romania
Reynai		
Risling (rejinski)	Beregivski (Italian 'Riesling')	Russia
	Paarl Riesling (Crouchen Blanc)	South Africa
JOHANNISBERG RIESLING	Emerald Riesling	USA
WHITE RIESLING	Gray Riesling (Pinot Gris)	
	Missouri Riesling (Hybrida Riparia × Vitis Labrusca)	
RIESLING RENANO		Argentina
RHINE RIESLING	HUNTER RIESLING (Sémillon)	Australia
	Clare Riesling (Crouchon)	
RHINE RIESLING		New Zealand

The History and Distribution of the Riesling Vine

The origin of the Riesling vine is uncertain, but the consensus among wine historians is that the variety developed from a wild vine in the German part of the Rhine valley somewhere between Koblenz and Worms during the Middle Ages.

Wine history is a murky discipline where national chauvinism has been a rather more important source of theories than rigorous academic research. In the middle of the last century the French historian Stoltz went to great lengths in his book *Ampélographie Rhénane* (Mulhouse, 1852) to prove that Riesling came eastwards to the Rhine valley from the Loire, though he could put forward only the most circumstantial evidence to support this obtuse theory.

The Austrians base their claim to being the Riesling vine's homeland on the record from the year 1301 of a vineyard named Ritzling near the village of Joching in the Wachau. Since there is a small stream close to Joching which even today bears the name Ritzlingbach, there would seem to be something in this story. However, there is nothing which suggests that the Ritzling vineyard was planted with Riesling vines in 1301.

To date, the earliest reliable record of the Riesling vine dates from 1435. It is an invoice written by the estate manager of the Count von Katzenellenbogen for Riesling vines planted that year in the Count's vineyards at Russelsheim on the river Main close to the Rheingau. This record is closely followed by one from Trier in the German part of the Mosel valley from the year 1465, and one from Worms in the Rheinhessen region of Germany from 1490.

The big step forward for Riesling came with the introduction of varietal monoculture – the planting of vineyards with a single grape variety – in Germany during the eighteenth century. In 1720–21, Schloss Johannisberg's vineyards in the Rheingau became the first Riesling monoculture. Because of their delicacy of aroma, Riesling wines don't show the typical character of the grape variety if even as little as 5 per cent of other aromatic varieties are blended with them.

Later in the eighteenth century Schloss Johannisberg again played a crucial role in the development of Riesling wine-making. There are many records of wines being made from rotten grapes in the Rheingau during the eighteenth century, but there was no consensus as to whether rot of any kind could result in better wines. In 1775 the harvest at Schloss Johannisberg was later than at any other estate in the region because the messenger carrying the instruction for the harvest to begin was delayed on his journey. By the time the estate manager, Johann Michael Engert, was able to start harvesting, 'rot' had set in. On 10 April 1776 he wrote, 'These 1775 wines in the seigneurial cellar receive such extraordinary approval from all manner of true connoisseurs, that you often hear nothing else said at tastings than: "I've never had such a wine in my mouth before."' The ability of noble rot to increase the quality of Riesling wines had been discovered.

From the 1783 vintage onwards, selective pickings for grapes affected by noble rot were made at Schloss Johannisberg. As the nineteenth century progressed more and more extreme selections of botrytized grapes were made by the aristocratic estates on the Rheingau, and the German system of designations for botrytized Riesling wines – Auslese, Beerenauslese, Trocken-beerenauslese – came into being.

The claim of the Mosel, Saar, and Ruwer valleys to an important place in Riesling's history as a noble variety is based on the decree by Clemens Wenzeslaus Prince-Bishop of Trier of 30 October 1787 that vines of inferior varieties planted along the Mosel valley should be grubbed up and replaced with 'good vines'. Official papers written by the Prince-Bishop's estate managers make it seem certain that the 'good vines' referred to were Riesling.

However, substantial replanting with Riesling on the Mosel didn't begin until after the secularization of the Church's enormous vineyards at the turn of the eighteenth and nineteenth centuries, and even then it wasn't until the end of the nineteenth century that Riesling became the dominant variety in the region. Late and selective harvesting came to the region relatively late. Auslese wines were first made towards the end of the last century, and Trockenbeerenausleses weren't made until the great 1921 vintage.

In Alsace, Riesling established itself as a variety of some importance only during the early part of this century, more than two centuries after its arrival in the region. In his *Dissertation du Vin* (Strasbourg, 1716) J. P. Jung describes Riesling as 'the new vine transported from the Rhine'. As late as 1893, in their *Handbuch des Weinbaues und der Kellerwirtschaft* (Berlin), Babo and Mach state that 'very little Riesling is to be found in Alsace'. It was only after Alsace reverted to French sovereignty in 1919 that high-quality wine production could be built up, and the Riesling acreage with it.

Babo and Mach also note that, excepting Germany and Alsace, 'Riesling is found most widely, but still only in isolated instances, in Lower Austria, Steiermark, Tyrol, and even more rarely in Hungary.' They were unaware that Riesling had already established modest footholds in California (1857), Washington State (1871), and South Australia (early 1880s) by this time. Undoubtedly, small plantations of Riesling also existed in Eastern European countries such as Romania and Yugoslavia by the end of the nineteenth century.

The arrival of Riesling in the vineyards of other important wine-producing countries is a twentieth-century phenomenon. German émigrés brought the Riesling vine to Chile, Argentina, and Brazil where it continues to be cultivated on a commercial scale (though the wines are best forgotten). The German training received by some Japanese and South Korean wine-makers spurred them to experiment with cultivating the Riesling vine in their homelands. In South Africa, New York State, and Canada a considered assessment of the climatic conditions in wine-growing areas made Riesling a logical choice for premium-quality wine production.

Serving and Storing Riesling Wines

FROM CELLAR TO GLASS

It is well known that fine red wines benefit from being stored
for several years, or even decades, in a cool, damp, dark cellar. It
is also widely accepted that when great red wines are brought to
the table they should be drunk from glasses with large bowls so
that the wine has a chance to 'breathe', and the bouquet can
fully develop. It is virtually unknown for the best Rieslings to be
treated in this manner, the reason being that so many wine
writers and wine merchants promote white wines as a vinous
source of 'instant gratification'. This is hardly helpful in per-
suading anyone of the true class of fine Riesling wines, many of
which can be every bit as aggressive in their youth and as
outstanding in maturity as top-class red wines.

Nevertheless, it should be stressed that simple-quality Riesling wines are best drunk during the first few years of their life.
Any wines given less than three stars in this book are not for
laying down, but for drinking before they are three or four
years old. They should then display a lively fruitiness and good
regional character, but they won't have the necessary structure
to develop extra complexity as a result of a long period of
maturation in the bottle. Wines with three or four stars will
definitely gain from at least five years' bottle ageing, and in
many cases from far longer. Five-star wines have the potential
to age for decades, and should be represented in every well-
stocked fine-wine cellar.

As a general rule Rieslings from the regions at the northern
extreme of viticulture in the Northern Hemisphere and from
regions close to the southern extreme of viticulture in the
Southern Hemisphere have the greatest ageing capacity, and
those from warmer regions where Riesling grapes don't have to
struggle to ripen are often best drunk young.

*

PERFECT AND SECOND-BEST STORAGE

Perfect storage conditions for Riesling wines aren't easy to come by in a world where modern building standards don't require subterranean cellars. The perfect cellar has a constant temperature of between 7° and 10°C, at least 70 per cent humidity, and is completely dark and free from vibration. If you are lucky enough to own a cellar like this, you can store fine Riesling wines here for just as long as the producer can in his own cellars.

A good second-best is the cupboard under the stairs, or any other dark corner where the temperature doesn't fluctuate too rapidly. The lack of such fluctuations is more important than a cool atmosphere, though it is certainly better if the temperature doesn't rise above 20°C. Here, wines will mature rather faster than in the perfect cellar. A wine stored here for two years will have matured as far as one stored in the perfect cellar for five or more years.

TEMPERATURE

The temperature at which Riesling wines are poured is critical to their enjoyment. Only the cheapest and most ordinary Rieslings should be served iced (i.e. below 7°C), and then only during hot weather. Better or top-quality Rieslings, whether dry or with some sweetness, should be drunk at cellar temperature. This is best achieved by bringing the wine to the table at about 7°/8°C, since it will rapidly warm a couple of degrees in the glass. Richer sweet and dessert Rieslings, along with Riesling wines which are well over ten years old, should be drunk slightly warmer – 12°C is ideal.

A young, top-quality Riesling is worth decanting, as the added contact of the wine with the air will really develop its aroma and flavour. However, the decanter should be lightly pre-chilled, or the wine will warm too rapidly. A quarter of an hour before drinking is normally enough time to allow it to 'breathe'.

The ideal glass for Riesling wines has a bowl not less than 8 cm high and 6 cm wide, and its form should lightly funnel the bouquet of the wine to the nose of the drinker. The perfect examples of this are the 'Young White Wine' glasses in the expensive Sommeliers series, and more modestly priced Vinum series, from the Austrian glass company Riedel. Also good and very reasonably priced is the larger white-wine glass in the Excelsior range from Schott-Zwiesel. The ISO standard tasting glass is also good.

Riesling Wines and Food

Riesling is one of the world's greatest wines for food.
David Rosengarten and Josh Wesson

If there was ever an ideal white 'food wine', it is Riesling. The lightness of body of most Riesling wines, combined with their vibrant fruitiness and palate-cleansing acidity, gives them the ideal balance to accompany an extremely wide range of dishes. The accepted idea that matching wines with food is all about putting together similar flavours doesn't stand up well to experiment or practice, while matching the balance of wines to the dominant flavours of particular dishes works very well. Looking at wine and food in this way, you find that Riesling wines are just made for today's lighter style of cooking. Their low alcoholic content, and extremely low calorific content, make them ideally suitable for the health-conscious and for weight-watchers.

Most savoury dishes contain meat, vegetables, and sauce components. Only rarely, in the case of hung beef or game, does the meat have the strongest flavour in a dish. Almost invariably it is the sauce which provides us with the more intense taste sensation. If the dish contains cheese of some kind, this is invariably the dominant component. The art of matching food and wine is to identify the strongest-tasting element(s) in a dish and find a wine which matches them well.

Since vegetables have a slight natural sweetness, and sauces gain a sweetness from caramelization or the cream or butter added to them, it follows that the wine should first of all match this sweetness. In dishes which contain only small amounts of vegetables or which aren't accompanied by a sauce, the wine must not overwhelm the subtle flavour of the meat, fish, or shellfish. Here it needs to be completely clean and without noticeable sweetness.

Rieslings of different kinds can fulfil both these roles beautifully. An off-dry Riesling with a refreshing acidity is the perfect match for dishes with a slightly sweet sauce. Its slight sweetness complements that of the sauce, and its acidity cuts its richness. Lighter, bone-dry Rieslings accompany very simply prepared meat, fish, or shellfish, since they don't dominate the food and always leave the mouth clean. High-alcohol wines tend to taste cloying if not matched against rich or spicy food. The intensity of the wine, be it red, white, Riesling, or Chardonnay, should always match that of the dish; subtly flavoured dishes require subtly flavoured wines.

Smoked meats and fish are a special case, since the smoke flavour tends to dominate and needs to be rounded off by the wine. If there is anything which spoils the harmony of smoked foods with wine it is the flavour of oak. The clash can be really ugly. A lighter, sweet-style Riesling, on the other hand, has a supple fruitiness which is perfectly set off by the flavour of smoke. A similar problem applies to soft white-rind cheeses, whose rind has a slightly bitter taste that also hates oak. Here a medium-bodied dry or off-dry Riesling cuts the fat of the cheese without accentuating the bitterness in its rind.

Rich, sweet Rieslings often have some problems with desserts, for if the sweetness of the dessert isn't exactly the same as that of the wine, the latter is thrown out of balance and the combination will taste sweet-sour. None the less, good combinations with certain fruit-based desserts can be made, and many dessert-style Riesling wines go well with blue cheeses and foie gras.

This is not to say that Riesling is a perfect food wine. It cannot generally cope with strongly spiced food, such as Hungarian and some kinds of Indian cuisine. Nor does it make a very happy match with Provençal or Italian dishes which contain a lot of garlic and olive oil.

GAZETTEER

KEY TO RATING SYSTEM

Quality

🍇 indifferent
🍇🍇 average
🍇🍇🍇 good
🍇🍇🍇🍇 very good
🍇🍇🍇🍇🍇 outstanding

Price

★ cheap
★★ average
★★★ expensive
★★★★ very expensive
★★★★★ luxury

AUSTRALIA

Total vineyard area: 165,000 acres
Vineyard area planted with Riesling: 6.5%/11,000 acres
Average annual Riesling production: 46,000,000 bottles

The Riesling vine has been in Australia for a little over a century. It is the most widely planted noble grape variety in Australia, and the acreage devoted to it is continuing to increase. More than anywhere else in the New World the variety and its wines are well established in Australia and seem to have a bright future well into the twenty-first century. There are many reasons for this, not the least of which are the large number of German immigrants who were instrumental in establishing the wine industry of Southern Australia, the relative simplicity of Riesling wine-making compared with wines of other noble varieties, and the 'Mediterranean' climate which Australia's major conurbations enjoy. The medium-bodied off-dry style of most Australian Riesling wines is made for this climate.

In Australia's export markets the lack of the climatic factor, and the image of Riesling as a sweet wine, have meant that sales of Chardonnay and Sauvignon Blanc varietal white wines have hitherto far exceeded those of Rieslings. However, there could be another reason for this. During the last decade Chardonnay has been the fashionable white-wine variety in Australia. It is with Chardonnay that wine-makers have tried to make their reputations, and with rare exceptions, such as Brian Croser of Petaluma in South Australia, few Australian wine-makers have invested much time in perfecting the making of Riesling wines. The result is that there are lots of pleasant, reasonably fruity Australian Riesling wines being produced today, but few really exciting ones.

GULF OF CARPENTARIA

CORAL SEA

RRITORY

QUEENSLAND

USTRALIA

PACIFIC OCEAN

Darling

Brisbane

NEW SOUTH WALES

S.A.CLARE-WATERVALE

S.A.BAROSSA VALLEY

Newcastle

Adelaide

Sydney

Wollongong

S.A. OUTHERN VALES

VICTORIA GOULBURN VALLEY

S.A.COONAWARRA

VICTORIA GREAT WESTERN

VICTORIA

Melbourne

TASMAN SEA

TASMANIA

Hobart

TASMANIA

Fifteen or twenty years ago things were very different. Then Riesling wasn't just a wine which sold easily, but one which could also make a wine-maker's reputation. The best Rieslings produced in Australia at this time, for example those from Leo Buring and Lindemans in South Australia, were superb wines that could be put up against the best from Alsace and Germany. They were made during the decade after Australian wine-makers had discovered how temperature-controlled fermentation and higher-altitude vineyards could produce white wines with more elegance. Most Australian wineries today regard their Rieslings as nothing more than 'cash-flow' wines, to be rushed into the bottle and onto the shelves as quickly as possible.

The one area in which Australian wine-makers have made significant progress with Riesling wine-making during the last decade is with dessert wines. Though Riesling wines from grapes affected by botrytis have been in Australia for twenty years it is only relatively recently that really impressive examples with the intense dried fruits and honeyed aromas and flavours of botrytis have been produced. These wines have neither quite the finesse nor the ageing potential of the finest Riesling dessert wines produced in Germany, but they make up for this with an opulent raisiny richness.

South Australia

Vineyard area planted with Riesling: 7,200 acres

Average annual Riesling production: 27,000,000 bottles

South Australia is by far the country's largest and most important Riesling wine-growing region, accounting for nearly 80 per cent of the country's production of Riesling wines. The greatest concentration of Riesling vineyards in the state is in the Barossa Valley, to the north-east of Adelaide. It is followed in importance by Clare Valley, about fifty miles to the north of the Barossa. The Adelaide Hills and the Southern Vales, the Lower Murray Valley, and Coonawarra in the extreme south-east of the state also have a significant Riesling wine production.

The dry, sappy style of Riesling wine traditionally produced here is the archetypal Australian Riesling. Medium-bodied, with 11.5° to 13° of alcohol, full citrusy aromas and flavours, and quite crisp acidity, the best examples are refreshing wines to drink young and can also age well. With bottle-maturation they take on the 'petrolly' character common to many mature Riesling wines, but also toasty, honeyed flavours quite distinct from those of any other Riesling wines. The dessert wines made from late-harvested Riesling grapes affected by botrytis are very rich, lusciously sweet wines, packed with honeyed fruit, many also having intense raisiny flavours. The best are capable of a decade of maturation in the bottle.

There are clear differences of character between the Riesling wines coming out of the various wine-growing regions in South Australia. The lightest and most floral come from Eden Valley and the hills above the Barossa Valley. Those from Coonawarra are medium-bodied and forthrightly fruity, and those from Clare are quite full-bodied, with fruit-salad aromas and flavours. The Barossa Valley itself produces full-bodied wines which often have a slight bitterness that many wine-makers cover with a touch of sweetness.

Since the early sixties wine-makers in the state have been actively pursuing greater elegance and delicacy of flavour in their Riesling wines. High-altitude vineyards have been planted by S. Smith & Son and Orlando, to name just two of the larger companies committed to Riesling. Night-picking has also been adopted by a number of wineries, since it results in crisper flavours and gives the wine-maker grapes which are cooler and therefore easier to work with. However, given the scale of Riesling wine production in this state, and the number of excellent Riesling wines that were made in South Australia during the sixties and seventies, it is disappointing that there aren't more exciting Rieslings coming out of the region's wineries today.

HEGGIES VINEYARD

See S. Smith & Son

HILL-SMITH

See S. Smith & Son

PETALUMA

Petaluma, Spring Gully Road, Piccadilly, S.A.

Estate bottled   20 acres of Riesling

150,000 bottles of Riesling per year

5,000 bottles of botrytis Riesling each suitable vintage

RHINE RIESLING

Quality: 🍇🍇🍇   Price: ★★★

BOTRYTIS RIESLING

Quality: 🍇🍇🍇🍇   Price: ★★★★

Best vintages: '80, '84, '85, '88

Forty-two-year-old Brian Croser is undoubtedly one of the most dynamic and sophisticated wine-makers in Australia and has received an extraordinary amount of acclaim since establishing Petaluma winery in the Adelaide Hills in 1978. However, he and his wines are also controversial. For his colleagues in Australia he is either a guru figure or second only to the devil, and his wines are alternately given rave reviews for their elegance and clarity or panned for being too neutral. A direct and outspoken wine-maker, Brian Croser does nothing to avoid becoming the object of such controversy.

In its crystal clarity and pure fruit flavours the Petaluma Rhine Riesling is a classic Croser wine. Although it is bone-dry, it has such a strong citrusy/fruit-salad character that it tastes as if it has a touch of sweetness. Released after some maturation in the bottle it is none the less extremely fresh and can mature further for many more years. The grapes are picked as soon as they reach optimum ripeness and given only the lightest of pressings. What then happens is truly remarkable. The grape juice is stored at minus 2°C for *five* months while Brian Croser is busy making other wines. Only then is the wine fermented, using Croser's own yeast cultures. It is bottled with minimal filtration, having been scrupulously protected from any contact with the air for the entirety of its life. However, in spite of all this wizardry some vintages of the Petaluma Rhine Riesling seem rather superficial, having plenty of aroma and up-front flavour, but too little structure.

The Petaluma botrytis Riesling, on the other hand, is one of the most impressive Riesling dessert wines made anywhere in the New World. It has great intensity of apricoty fruit, with a subtle spiciness from botrytis, and excellent length of flavour. The balance of sweetness and acidity is near perfect, and the wine has more finesse than any other made in this style in Australia. It is made in vintages only when enough botrytis develops on the grapes (so far 1981, '84, '85, '88).

PEWSEY VALE

See S. Smith & Son

S. SMITH & SON

| S. Smith & Son, P.O. Box 10, 5353 Angaston, S.A.

Heggies Vineyard

| Estate bottled

| 120,000 bottles of Rhine Riesling per year

| 8,000 bottles of botrytis Riesling per year

| RHINE RIESLING

| Quality: 🍇🍇   Price: ★★★

| BOTRYTIS RIESLING

| Quality: 🍇🍇🍇🍇   Price: ★★★★

Pewsey Vale

Estate bottled

240,000 bottles of Riesling per year

Quality: 🍇🍇🍇   Price: ★★★

Hill-Smith 'Old Triangle' Riesling

240,000 bottles of Riesling per year

Quality: 🍇🍇   Price: ★★

Best vintages: '82, '84, '87, '89

S. Smith & Son are one of the few larger wine producers in South Australia wholeheartedly committed to the Riesling vine. For more than twenty years they have been acquiring and developing high-altitude vineyard sites in the Adelaide Hills above the Barossa Valley, ideal for producing premium-quality Riesling wines. This has meant huge investments, most notably in the replanting of the Pewsey Vale vineyard site in 1961 and in establishing Heggies Vineyard from 1971.

The Heggies Vineyard Rhine Riesling is the top of the S. Smith & Son range of dry Rieslings, and there can be no doubting that wine-maker Alan Hoey sets strict standards in its production. However, for all its mouth-filling lemony fruit it often comes across as rather heavy. The Pewsey Vale Rhine Riesling is much more attractive, with an appealing flowery bouquet, ripe citrusy fruit and some real elegance. The Hill-Smith 'Old Triangle' Riesling is a good wine for its price bracket and is made in a medium-dry Germanic style. With slightly lower alcohol than either the Heggies Vineyard or Pewsey Vale wines it is quite crisp and has a nice fresh fruiti-ness, though the flavours are quite short and simple.

In a completely different class is the Heggies Vineyard botrytis Riesling. It is a stunning wine, its bouquet packed with every sort of fruit imaginable, and plenty of spice from botrytis. It makes a huge impression in the mouth, but is still cleaner and more elegant than the majority of wines in this style from Australia; certainly a very sweet wine, but one in which the sweetness is by no means dominant.

Tasmania

Vineyard area planted with Riesling: 35 acres

Average annual Riesling production: 42,000 bottles

The search for cooler-climate vineyard sites which can produce more delicately flavoured wines which has been under way in Australia since the early sixties inevitably led to Tasmania. It is the most southerly state in Australia, and its climate is a mild maritime one. As yet there are only a handful of commercial wine producers on the island, but already some very promising results have been achieved with Riesling.

MOORILLA ESTATE

Moorilla Estate, 655 Main Road, Berriedale 7011, Tasmania

Estate bottled   17 acres of Riesling

30,000 bottles of Riesling per year

Quality: 🍇🍇🍇   Price: ★★★

Best vintages: '88, '89

Julian Alcorso's Moorilla Estate, situated just outside Tasmania's capital, Hobart, is the most important producer of Riesling wines on the island. Although the island's climate is cool he produces an intensely fruity dry Riesling wine which shows complex over-ripe pear and peach aromas and flavours. Yields in Tasmania are very low, and this combined with careful vineyard management enables Julian Alcorso to harvest grapes with a high degree of physiological ripeness. Although not very high in alcohol, it is a full-bodied, mouth-filling wine that can accompany quite spicy food, though on account of its richness it also drinks well on its own.

Victoria

Vineyard area planted with Riesling: 950 acres

Average annual Riesling production: 4,000,000 bottles

Riesling plays a much smaller part in the very diverse wine production of the State of Victoria than it does in South Australia, yet some of the best and most interesting Riesling wines produced in the country today come from here. The best Victorian Riesling wines made to date pack a big punch of fruit and have plenty of alcohol behind it. They are the heavy artillery of Australian Riesling, and not for those seeking lightness and delicacy. In spite of their huge aroma and mouth-filling flavours when young, they have good ageing potential and can be as delightful at ten years of age as at one. The older they get the more elegance they acquire.

MICHELTON

Michelton Vintners, Mitchelton, Nagambie 3608, Victoria

120,000 bottles of Riesling per year

RHINE RIESLING

Quality: ♥♥♥♥   Price: ★★★

BOTRYTIS-AFFECTED RHINE RIESLING

Quality: ♥♥♥   Price: ★★★★

Best vintages: '80, '81, '83, '85, '86, '88, '89

Michelton's Rhine Riesling, made from fruit from the Goulburn Valley, is quite simply the best dry Riesling wine being produced in Australia today. It has a concentration of flavour and intensity of aroma greater than any other wine in this class. To taste it is to learn just how great Australian dry Riesling can be, and to see just how badly most Australian

Riesling producers are currently underachieving. It has a huge bouquet of citrus and exotic fruits that leaps out of the glass at you, and the wine is mouth-fillingly rich in spite of being almost bone-dry. Its often high alcoholic content hardly shows, thanks to the excellent balance of fruit, acidity, and alcohol.

The Michelton vineyard was founded in 1969, and the first wines produced in 1974. This ambitious venture, including a winery with a tower over 150 feet high, ran into financial problems, though. Finally, it came into the ownership of the Valmorbida family. Since the late seventies its wines have won stacks of medals and been highly praised in the international wine press. From the beginning, one of its specialities has been dry Riesling, and every one of the Riesling wines made by wine-maker Don Lewis has been a trophy or gold-medal winner.

The winery's botrytis-affected Riesling dessert wine is also fine, with an excellent depth of peachy-citrusy fruit, but comes across as rather sweet and one-sided – a good wine to enjoy with slightly sweet fruit desserts, but with not quite enough structure to be classed as outstanding. Small quantities of older vintages of the dry Rhine Riesling are sometimes released under the Mitchelton Classic Release label. These are remarkably fresh and elegant.

MOUNT CHALAMBAR

Mt Chalambar Wines, Box 301, Ararat 3377, Victoria

Estate bottled

6,000 bottles of Riesling per year

Quality: 🍇🍇🍇   Price: ★★★

Best vintages: '86, '88, '89

Young wine-maker Trevor Mast's small winery in the Great Western area of Victoria produces some of the most elegant, floral Rieslings in the state. Medium-bodied and almost bone-dry, they have plenty of confectionery fruit character and are very clean, with a crisp finish. Trevor Mast's German training, at the famous Geisenheim wine school, shows through strongly in these wines, which in spite of their dryness have a distinctly Germanic character to them. His wine-making methods are designed to reduce the handling of his wines to the absolute minimum.

As well as making wine from his own vineyard on Mount Chalambar, Trevor Mast is also wine-maker at Mount Langi Ghiran Vineyards, where he makes a very different, much spicier, style of Riesling wine.

Western Australia

Vineyard area planted with Riesling: 500 acres
Average annual Riesling production: 1,000,000 bottles

Western Australia's wines have shot to stardom during the last few years, though it is actually nearly twenty years since the state's first top-quality wines were produced in the Margaret River. Here, immediately behind Cape Mentelle, south of Perth, and at Mt Barker, 150 miles further south and east, are excellent cooler-climate viticultural regions capable of producing wines from the noble grape varieties that can challenge the best of Europe. While it is the Chardonnay white wines and Cabernet Sauvignon red wines which have captured the headlines, the Riesling vine can also produce extremely attractive wines here. They are considerably crisper and more elegant than those of South Australia and have a rather more subtle character than the majority of Rieslings from Victoria.

PLANTAGENET

Plantagenet Wines, P.O. Box 122, Mt Barker 6324, W.A.

Estate bottled   15 acres of Riesling

42,000 bottles of Riesling per year

Quality: 🍇🍇🍇   Price: ★★★

Best vintages: '86, '88

Plantagenet was the first commercial producer of off-dry Ries-ling wines in the Mt Barker area of Western Australia. The founding partners were sheep and cattle farmers Anthony Smith, who now manages the winery, and Michael Meredith-Hardy. They planted their first vineyards simultaneously with the state government's experimental plantations in 1968, and their first Riesling vines went into the ground in 1971. Their Riesling vineyards are situated on the southern slopes of Mt Barker on free-draining gravelly loam soil. They bring elegant medium-bodied Rieslings with crisp well-defined lemony pas-sion-fruit flavours and a nice 'spritz' of carbon dioxide. The latter comes from the very long cool fermentation and helps the wine to taste much lighter in alcohol than it actually is. It benefits from several years' maturation in the bottle and will keep for a decade.

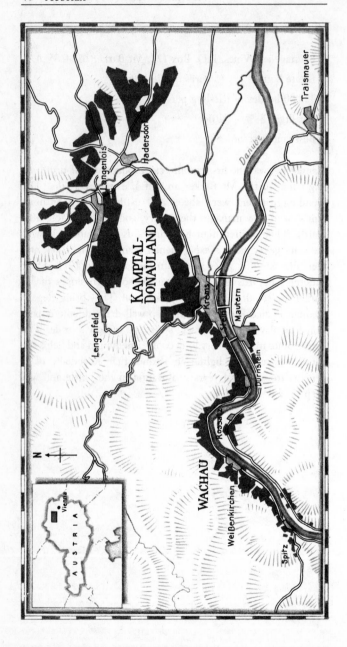

AUSTRIA

Total vineyard area: 145,000 acres
Vineyard area planted with Riesling: 2%/2,750 acres
Average annual Riesling production: 10,000,000 bottles

No Riesling wines are more underrated than those of Austria. The quality of the dry Riesling wines produced here can be matched only by the very top producers of Alsace and the Rheinpfalz region in Germany. Indeed, they are among the finest dry white wines produced anywhere in the world, and they possess an impressive richness of fruit together with great elegance and minerally complexity. Compared with the majority of Alsace Rieslings they taste less alcoholic, crisper, and more forthrightly fruity. Tasted against fine dry German Rieslings they are fuller-bodied, more aromatic, and generally have a better harmony owing to their softer acidity. Yet these world-class wines are virtually unknown to wine drinkers outside Austria itself.

The reason for this is very simple. Austria's name as a fine-wine-producing nation remains tainted by the diethylene-glycol, or 'anti-freeze', scandal of 1985. However, anyone who takes the trouble to taste a range of the best dry white, red, or dessert wines produced in Austria today will surely agree that it is high time this scandal was forgotten. Austria now deserves to be taken as seriously as any other wine-producing nation in Europe. Though the glycol scandal created great image problems for Austrian wines in the English-speaking world, it greatly stimulated the development of the domestic market for high-quality Austrian wines. A decade ago the top Riesling producers of Austria already made some superb wines, but they could virtually be counted on one hand. The increased demand within Austria for high-quality estate-bottled wines since 1985 has encouraged many more producers to work for the highest possible quality.

The only problem which faces Austria's Riesling wines in gaining greater international recognition is the limited quantity of wine available. Of the 2,750 acres of Riesling vineyards in Austria, less than a quarter lie in regions where both soil and climate offer the chance to produce top-quality wines. Owing to the voracious domestic demand, many of the top producers are sold out of Riesling wines before the new vintage is even bottled! Luckily, in the regions best suited to the Riesling vine the variety accounts for only a small proportion of the vineyard area. As vineyards are replanted the proportion of them stocked with Riesling will increase dramatically, and by the next century Riesling should become the dominant variety in the Wachau and the more favoured parts of Kamptal–Donauland.

Kamptal–Donauland

Total vineyard area: 16,065 acres

Vineyard area planted with Riesling: 775 acres

Average annual Riesling production: 240,000 bottles

Kamptal–Donauland, though a relatively small wine-producing region, has an extremely diverse landscape, producing equally diverse wines. On its eastern border are terraced vineyards on steep mountain slopes, while Langenlois, its largest wine-producing commune, is set in rolling countryside where agriculture and wine-growing stand side by side. Seen statistically, the Riesling vine plays a minor role here. However, it is concentrated in three areas where it produces wines of extremely high quality. These wines are among the region's most renowned products, and are therefore of disproportionate importance.

The most important of these is the great Heiligenstein vineyard of Zöbing, close to Langenlois. Its south-facing slopes, with an inclination of around 30 degrees, and its stony volcanic and weathered sandstone soil produce Riesling wines every bit as fine as those of the Wachau. They are extremely aromatic, firmly structured, and racy.

Completely different in style are the wines from the villages close to the Danube to the east of Krems. Here the Riesling vine grows on deep loess soils, giving quite full-bodied wines, often with earthy/vegetal aromas and flavours.

The third Riesling stronghold in the region, the vineyards of the small town of Stein and those on the western side of Krems, is described in the section on the Wachau, since its wines are virtually identical with those of that region.

JURTSCHITSCH

> Weingut Jurtschitsch-Sonnhof, Rudolfstrasse 39, 3550 Langenlois
>
> Estate bottled   10.5 acres of Riesling
>
> 24,000 bottles of Riesling per year
>
> Quality: 🍇🍇🍇   Price: ★★★ – ★★★★
>
> Best vintages: '71, '73, '79, '81, '85, '86, '88, '90

Brothers Dr Karl, Edwin, and Paul Jurtschitsch run a model wine estate in Langenlois with great professionalism, each having responsibility for a different side of the estate's management. Their vineyards, largely situated in the best sites of Langenlois, are cultivated organically, though the Jurtschitsches would shy somewhat at being described as 'organic' wine producers. The majority of the Riesling vineyards are situated in the Heiligenstein, Seeberg, and Loiser Berg sites whose stony volcanic soils bring very low yields.

The estate's wine-making is unashamedly modern, with temperature-controlled fermentation in stainless-steel tanks for all the white wines. This makes for dry Rieslings with an intense clean fruitiness and crisp acidity. The best are the Cabinet and Spätlese wines from the Heiligenstein, which have a considerable minerally depth and considerable elegance.

MANTLERHOF

> Weingut Mantlerhof, Hauptstrasse 50, 3494 Brunn im Felde
>
> Estate bottled   3 acres of Riesling
>
> 9,000 bottles of Riesling per year
>
> Quality: 🍷🍷🍷   Price: ★★★
>
> Best vintages: '77, '79, '83, '86, '88, '89, '90

Young Sepp Mantler runs one of the oldest and the most modern wine estates in Kamptal–Donauland. The estate, which also cultivates 135 acres of agricultural land, has been in the ownership of Sepp Mantler's family since at least 1365. He is one of the most forthright advocates of modern wine-making in the region, fermenting his wines exclusively in stainless-steel tanks and using wooden casks only to mature and soften wines with a high acidity. His dry Rieslings are extremely lively, with a vivid fruitiness and crisp acidity, which retain their youthful freshness for a long time. Thanks to their deep, compact soils his vineyards in Gedersdorf rarely suffer from drought problems, and he frequently produces rich Riesling wines of Spätlese or Auslese quality. These are always fermented dry, to give wines with considerable power.

MARIA RETZL

> Weingut Maria Retzl, Heiligensteinstrasse 9, 3561 Zöbing
>
> Estate bottled   12.5 acres of Riesling
>
> 24,000 bottles of Riesling per year
>
> Quality: 🍷🍷🍷🍷🍷   Price: ★★★ – ★★★★
>
> Best vintages: '71, '73, '75, '77, '79, '81, '83, '85, '86, '88, '90

While some of the Wachau wine-makers have a reputation which extends beyond the borders of their country, I doubt if anyone outside the German-speaking world has heard of Maria Retzl. Yet she produces some of the most remarkable dry Riesling wines in the whole of Austria. Her estate was founded more than a century ago by Ferdinand Mantler, who was honoured for his Riesling wines as early as 1890. At the turn of the century, he was one of the very first Austrian wine-growers to bottle his own wines. The estate then passed by inheritance to the Hiesinger family, and twenty years ago Maria Retzl, *née* Hiesinger, suddenly found herself running the family estate after the death of her husband. In spite of having received no training she has maintained the very high-quality standards set by previous generations, and is now preparing her son Erwein to take over the estate.

The Retzl Riesling wines are easily the richest and most concentrated produced from the great Heiligenstein site of Zöbing. They are extremely aromatic, and in spite of their mouth-filling apricoty fruit, substantial body, and mineral extract are always very elegant. The grapes are late-harvested for the highest possible degree of ripeness, and because of the policy of declassifying Riesling Kabinett wines (the normal quality produced by the estate) wine may have as much as 13° of natural alcohol!

The Retzls' cellar is cut deep into the side of the Heiligenstein. In the small wood-panelled tasting-room hang numerous prizes and honours bestowed on Ferdinand Mantler and Dr Hiesinger. A tasting here is an unforgettable experience. As one great wine follows another you repeatedly ask yourself how the next wine can be any better, but invariably it is.

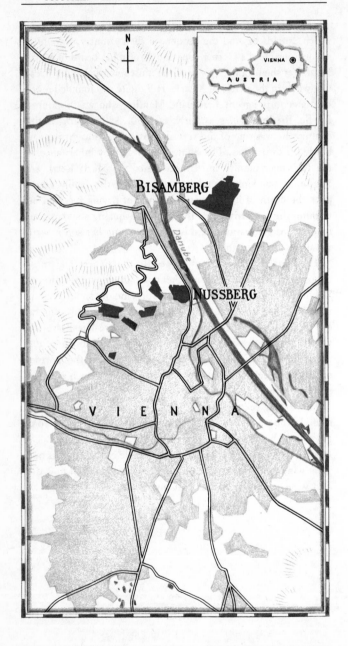

Vienna

Total vineyard area: 1,700 acres

Vineyard area planted with Riesling: 8%/140 acres

Average annual Riesling production: 360,000 bottles

Though both Paris and Berlin are proud of their token vineyards, Vienna is the only European metropolis which is a significant wine producer. Viticulture was already established here by the time the Romans arrived in the first century A D. By the end of the last century Vienna had established itself as a quality wine-producing region, and the grape varieties which make up the larger part of the vineyard area today, Riesling, Grüner Veltliner, Weissburgunder, and Traminer, were well established.

The Vienna wine culture is given a unique character by the wine-growers' taverns, or *Heurige*, through which the larger part of the city's wine production is sold. There are nearly two hundred of these, and they can be found in all the wine-growing suburbs of the city: Nussdorf, Kahlenbergdorf, Heiligenstadt, Grinzing, Sievering, Neustift, and on the left bank of the Danube in Stammersdorf, Strebersdorf, and Jedlersdorf. The majority of wines served here are of simple quality, without any indication of grape variety. Only the better wines are bottled, and these can be very fine indeed. However, they are rare – only thirty wine-growers in the city sell bottled wines.

Arguably the finest Vienna wines are the Rieslings from the Nussberg in the 19th Bezirk of the city, and those from the slopes of the Bisamberg above Strebersdorf and Stammersdorf on the left bank of the Danube. Both these sites have an excellent southerly exposition and benefit from the warming influence of the nearby Danube. Neither wine is as immediately attractive in its youth as a Riesling wine from the Wachau or Kamptal–Donauland. However, after a few years in the bottle they can make wines of considerable character and elegance.

FRANZ MAYER

Mayer am Pfarrplatz, Beethovenhaus, Pfarrplatz 2, 1190 Wien

Estate bottled   21 acres of Riesling

36,000 bottles of Riesling per year

Quality: 🍇🍇🍇   Price: ★★★

Best vintages: '71, '75, '79, '81, '82, '86, '88, '90

Franz Mayer is the most important producer of Vienna Riesling wines, both in terms of quantity and because he makes the finest Riesling wines from the excellent Nussberg site of Nussdorf. He now runs the seventy-five-acre estate with his stepson Mario Galler, who came to Vienna from another famous Riesling wine-producing region, the Barossa Valley in South Australia, in 1980. They make an unusual but seemingly harmonious duo.

Of the two dry Riesling wines made by the Mayer estate that from the Alsegger vineyard, of which they are the sole owners, is the more ordinary. It is light and bone-dry, rather tart and short of flavour in lesser vintages, but with an attractive apricoty fruit in better years. The Nussberg Riesling is considerably more powerful, with concentrated peachy fruit, and is just off-dry. It combines full peachy fruit and elegant acidity, continuing to improve in the bottle for as much as a decade, and is capable of lasting for considerably longer.

The Mayers' house is an important historical landmark in Vienna, for it was here in 1808 that Beethoven wrote a large part of his 6th (Pastoral) Symphony while taking the waters in Heiligenstadt, which he hoped would relieve his increasing deafness. Perhaps he would have been cured if he had drunk Nussberg Riesling instead of Heiligenstadt water! The *Heurige* which it houses today is open from 10 January until 20 December, and music is provided by a traditional *Schrammelmusik* trio.

*

WIENINGER

> Weingut Ing. Wieninger, Stammersdorfer Strasse 78, 1210
> Wien
>
> Estate bottled   1 acre of Riesling
>
> 3,000 bottles of Riesling per year
>
> Quality: 🍇🍇🍇🍇   Price: ★★★
>
> Best vintages: '77, '79, '83, '86, '88, '90

Ing. Wieninger is by far the smallest producer to appear in this guide, yet it would be too sad to overlook what are easily the finest Riesling wines from the Bisamberg site on the left bank of the Danube. Avoidance of chemical fertilization, and conservative wine-making in wooden casks with minimal filtration, enable Friedrich Wieninger Snr and Jr to produce Riesling wines with intense peachy fruit, elegance, and charm. They are one of only a handful of estates in the city with a reputation that extends beyond its boundaries.

The Wieninger *Heurige* is open 15 January–15 July, then 15 August–15 December, except on Mondays. An Austrian wine tour would be incomplete without an evening here.

Wachau

> Total vineyard area: 3,350 acres
>
> Vineyard area planted with Riesling: 8%/275 acres
>
> Average annual Riesling production: 720,000 bottles

The Wachau is one of the world's most beautiful wine landscapes. Along a stretch of the river Danube roughly ten miles in length, vines cling to small terraces, often wide enough for only two or three rows of vines, which cover the steep rocky mountain-sides up to an altitude of over 600 feet above the Danube.

From here there are spectacular views across the river valley to the forests which cover the slopes above the right, north-facing, bank. At Dürnstein is the massive rocky crag of the Biratalwand, on which perches the ruined fortress where Richard the Lionheart was imprisoned. The town looks as if it has barely changed since then.

The Riesling wines of the region fully reflect both the rocki-ness of the landscape and the warm climate which the closed valley and large expanse of the Danube give it. Almost all the Riesling vineyards are situated on terraces with a stony volcanic (Gneiss) soil, and those situated on flat ground lie directly at the base of the mountain-sides. This extremely free-draining soil, and the influence of the cool air which flows down into the Danube valley from the mountains above, give the wines their elegance and finesse. The warm sunny summers and autumns allow the grapes to reach a high degree of ripeness, giving them their aromatic richness.

Wine-making in the Wachau is extremely traditional. There is hardly a single producer who doesn't mature all his wines in wooden casks for at least a few months, and the majority of producers make and mature them exclusively in wood. At the best estates very little is done to the wines beyond the minimum of filtration necessary to clarify them. This, and the low yields enforced by the dry climate of the region, result in an intensity and finesse that few dry white wines anywhere in the world can match.

Almost all the wine-growers in the Wachau, including the regional co-operative, which produces 40 per cent of all Wachau wine, are members of the Vinea Wachau Nobilis Dis-trictus. This association has created a classification system for the region's wines quite unlike any other. The 'lowest' category is Steinfeder, which is for light bone-dry wines with a maximum of 10.7° of alcohol. Then comes Federspiel, which is the most typical style for Wachau Riesling wines. They are medium-bodied and dry, with ripe fruit flavours and an elegant balance of alcohol, fruit, and acidity. The top category is Smaragd, which are full-bodied, rich dry and off-dry wines with 12° of alcohol or more.

Steinfeder Riesling wines are ideal for drinking young with light food, or for enjoying by themselves in warm weather. Federspiel Rieslings are perfect with fish, meat dishes with light sauces, and creamy cheeses. Smaragd wines have enough body and depth of flavour to handle fatty meats and poultry in rich sauces. With each step up the scale the ageing potential of the wines increases, and Smaragd wines from the best producers are capable of maturing in the bottle for several decades.

FRANZ HIRTZBERGER

Weingut Franz Hirtzberger, Kremser Strasse 8, 3620 Spitz

Estate bottled   6 acres of Riesling

15,000 bottles of Riesling per year

Quality: 🍇🍇🍇🍇🍇   Price: ★★★ – ★★★★

Best vintages: '71, '73, '75, '77, '79, '82, '83, '86, '88, '89, '90

Franz Hirtzberger Jr makes the most elegant Riesling wines in the Wachau. Together with his energetic wife Irmgard he runs the finest wine estate in Spitz, the most westerly of the Wachau's wine-growing villages. In large part it is the special climate of Spitz, which is more strongly influenced by cool air streams from the surrounding mountains than other parts of the region, that is responsible for the racy brilliance and vivid fruitiness of the Hirtzberger Riesling wines.

A highly intelligent, thoughtful man, Franz Hirtzberger is President of the Wachau wine producers' association Vinea Wachau Nobilis Districtus. Since he took over running the estate in 1983 he has followed the conservative path established by his father during the seventies, but has added a few import-ant refinements (fermentation in stainless-steel tanks, and malolactic fermentation to soften the steely acidity of the wines from lesser vintages). Because of the cool micro-climate of Spitz he waits as long as possible before harvesting. The Ries-ling grapes are rarely picked before the second week in November.

The best vineyard site in Spitz is the steep terraced Singer-riedel immediately behind the village. In the best vintages Franz Hirtzberger's Riesling wines from this site are perhaps the greatest in the entire region. The neighbouring Hochrain vineyard also produces fine Rieslings in good vintages, which are slightly broader in character because of the deeper soil. In the wines from these sites vibrant acidity is perfectly married to intense apricot and exotic fruit in what can only be described as a scintillating taste explosion.

Because of their combination of crispness and intense fruiti-ness the Hirtzberger Rieslings make excellent food wines. This fact hasn't escaped the attention of Austria's numerous top restaurants, and hot demand from them makes these wonderful wines very hard to obtain.

JOSEF JAMEK

Weingut Josef Jamek, 3610 Joching 45

Estate bottled   21.5 acres of Riesling

60,000 bottles of Riesling per year

Quality: 🍷🍷🍷🍷   Price: ★★★ – ★★★★

Best vintages: '71, '73, '75, '77, '79, '83, '86, '88, '89

Without the pioneering work of Josef Jamek the Wachau might never have established itself as a premier wine-producing region. He began building up the Jamek wine estate immedi-ately after he returned to Joching from the war late in 1945. '1946 and '47 were excellent vintages, and wines more or less made themselves,' he told me during a recent visit, 'then in 1948 we all began adding sugar to the wines to build them up [to increase their alcoholic content]. In 1960 I made the decision to abandon this, and to stop making any sweet wines. With these new-style wines I started to find customers among Austria's best hotels and restaurants. It wasn't many years before some of my near neighbours such as Herr Prager in Weissenkirchen and Herr Knoll in Loiben were taking a similar path, which has finally led to the Wachau's success today.'

While the great majority of wine producers in the Wachau have followed Josef Jamek's lead in abandoning the addition of sugar to their wines, and in fermenting them all through to dryness, his use of malolactic fermentation remains controversial. It makes Josef Jamek's Riesling wines atypically soft and silky in flavour. Tasted in direct comparison with other Wachau Rieslings they can seem a little flat, but they have a wonderful richness of fruit. The estate's finest Riesling wines are those from the Klaus site of Weissenkirchen, where Josef Jamek has ten acres of Riesling vines. The dry stone walls of its steep terraces are maintained by four full-time workers of the Jamek estate.

As if his sixty-acre wine estate didn't give him enough to do, Josef Jamek also runs a superb restaurant in Joching. Such is his commitment to maintaining the highest possible standards here that it is very rare indeed not to find him at his restaurant when it is open.

EMMERICH KNOLL

Weingut Emmerich Knoll, 3601 Unterloiben 10

Estate bottled   5 acres of Riesling

15,000 bottles of Riesling per year

Quality: 🍷🍷🍷🍷🍷   Price: ★★★ – ★★★★

Best vintages: '71, '73, '75, '77, '79, '83, '86, '88, '90

Emmerich Knoll makes some of the most richly fruity dry Riesling wines anywhere in the world. A modest and reserved man of devout Catholic persuasion, he would undoubtedly greet such a judgement with great astonishment, and attribute the larger part of the responsibility for the quality of his wines to the vineyards. It is certainly true that Loiben has the warmest micro-climate in the entire Wachau, and that this results in Riesling wines with a mouth-filling succulence and an extremely full aroma. Loiben Riesling wines can sometimes be rather clumsy and a little alcoholic though, a fault which never afflicts any of Herr Knoll's wines even when they have more than 12° of alcohol. Instead, they have just as much refinement as they do richness.

Herr Knoll's Riesling vineyards lie predominantly in two such steep terraced sites: the Loibenberg of Loiben, and the Pfaffenberg of Stein (technically part of the neighbouring Kamptal–Donauland region). Both produce superb wines, the Pfaffenberg having a pronounced peachiness. However, his top Riesling site is the virtually flat Schütt, situated in a sheltered hollow at the base of the mountains between Loiben and Dürnstein. The Schütt wines have an extremely intense bouquet of cassis and exotic fruits, and the greatest ageing potential of all the Knoll Riesling wines.

The wines of the Emmerich Knoll estate are instantly recognizable on the shelf because of the estate's extremely florid label depicting St Urban. With characteristic quiet determination Emmerich Knoll has no intention whatsoever of changing it for something more modern.

NIKOLAIHOF

Weingut Nikolaihof, Nikolaigasse 77, 3512 Mautern

Estate bottled   14 acres of Riesling

30,000 bottles of Riesling per year

STEINER HUND RIESLING

Quality: 🍇🍇🍇🍇🍇   Price: ★★★★

OTHER RIESLINGS

Quality: 🍇🍇🍇🍇   Price: ★★★★

Best vintages: '71, '75, '73, '77, '79, '83, '86, '88, '90

Nikolaus and Christine Saahs run one of the oldest and greatest wine estates in Austria. Mautern was one of the largest Roman towns in Austria during the first century A D, and it was then that the first vineyards were planted on the right bank of the

Danube. The first mention of the Nikolaihof, which was home to the monastic foundation of St Nikolaus for eight centuries, dates from 1073, though the buildings erected during the eleventh century were almost certainly built on old Roman foundations. Since 1894 it has been in the possession of the Saahs family.

Nikolaus Saahs's wines are definitely not for those seeking instant sensual gratification. They are the most highly structured wines of the entire Wachau, and are made for long ageing, using ultra-conservative methods. These begin in the vineyards, where the average age of the vines is nearly thirty years. No chemical fertilizers are used, and virtually no chemical spraying is done. The grapes for the best wines are still pressed using a century-old wooden press nearly forty feet in length. All his wines are matured in wooden casks.

The finest, and also the most extreme in style, of the Nikolaihof dry Riesling wines are those from the Steiner Hund site (technically part of Kamptal–Donauland rather than the Wachau). Tasted very young they have a great intensity of flavour, combined with an almost biting acidity. They develop extremely slowly, but after two years' maturation in the bottle they begin to show their minerally complexity of aroma and flavour. After ten or so years of ageing they come to their peak, displaying truly awesome power and length on the palate.

The estate buildings occupy all four sides of a large courtyard which is dominated by a huge lime tree. On one side of the courtyard is the eleventh-century chapel, which has been converted to a 'knights' hall' where tastings for larger groups are held, and on the opposite side is the estate's excellent wine bar. Open from the beginning of March until the end of June and from the beginning of September until mid-December, it is an essential part of the programme for any visitor to the region.

FRANZ XAVIER PICHLER

Weingut Franz Xavier Pichler, 3601 Oberloiben 27

Estate bottled   2.5 acres of Riesling

8,000 bottles of Riesling per year

Quality: 🍇🍇🍇🍇🍇   Price: ★★★ – ★★★★

Best vintages: '71, '77, '79, '86, '88, '89

Step by step Franz Xavier Pichler has improved his wine-making until he numbers among the very top wine-makers of the region. In 1981 he abandoned the chemical fertilization of the vineyards and the chaptalization of the wines, and in 1985 he abandoned using fining agents to clarify the wines in the cellar. Filtration has also been reduced, and all the wines are fermented and matured in wooden casks.

The Pichler Rieslings are extremely elegant, classical dry wines with a pronounced acidity that is often masked by the wines' sheer intensity of fruit and extract. His Rieslings from the Dürnsteiner Kellerberg, in particular, are very concentrated, rich wines with an extremely long aftertaste. Because of the quality of this site and Herr Pichler's policy of late-harvesting, they are almost invariably produced in the Smaragd style, the highest-quality grade for dry Wachau Riesling wines. Slightly lighter, but also very fine, are the Riesling wines from the Steinertal site of Loiben.

FRANZ PRAGER

Weingut Franz Prager, 3610 Weissenkirchen 48

Estate bottled   12.5 acres of Riesling

36,000 bottles of Riesling per year

Quality: 🍇🍇🍇🍇   Price: ★★★ – ★★★★

Best vintages: '71, '73, '75, '77, '79, '83, '86, '88

Franz Prager and his stepson Anton Bodenstein make some of the most structured wines in the Wachau. Because of their pronounced acidity they are far from being the most immediately appealing wines of the region. However, after two or three years of maturation in the bottle they become wonderfully racy dry Rieslings in which power is matched with finesse.

The Prager family have owned vineyards in Weissenkirchen since 1715. Herr Prager was one of the first wine-growers in the region to start producing high-quality dry wines from Riesling and Grüner Veltliner (a traditional Austrian variety) during the 1950s. His best Riesling wines come from the extremely steep, terraced Steinriegel site, which occupies a south-west-facing slope in a sheltered side valley. Here the soil is still ploughed by horses, and all other work is done entirely by hand. All the Riesling wines are fermented in wood in the extensive cellars under the Pragers' home. Every barrel is bottled separately, and the wines are consequently of great individuality.

Though the estate's Riesling wines, in common with those of the Wachau generally, are fermented to dryness, Franz Prager is one of only a handful of wine producers in the region who make dessert wines when conditions permit. They are only slightly sweet, their sweetness coming just from the grape sugar which the yeast has been unable to ferment to alcohol. Both the 1969 and 1979 vintage Riesling Auslese are sensational wines that are quite the equal of the best Riesling dessert wines from Germany.

FRITZ SALOMON

Fritz Salomon K.G. – Weingut Undhof, Undstrasse 10, 3504 Krems–Stein

Estate bottled   17 acres of Riesling

36,000 bottles of Riesling per year

Quality: 🍇🍇🍇   Price: ★★★

Best vintages: '71, '73, '75, '77, '79, '81, '83, '86, '88, '90

There is nothing flashy or inflated about Erich Salomon, but he makes some of the best dry Riesling wines from three top vineyard sites which through an accident of history belong politically to the region of Kamptal–Donauland, but produce wines which are 100 per cent Wachau in character. These are the Kremser Kögl, the Steiner Hund, and Steiner Pfaffenberg. All are steep terraced vineyards with the same volcanic Gneiss soil as that of the Wachau proper.

Erich Salomon's ancestors, who originated from South Tyrol, bought the monastic Undhof estate in the town of Stein in 1792. Towards the end of the 1920s, his father, Fritz, was one of the first wine producers in Austria to bottle his own wines. He also planted the estate's first Riesling vines, which he brought from Geisenheim in the Rheingau, where he had studied. Erich Salomon, who took over the estate in 1971 after the death of his father, continues the estate's traditional style of wine-making. Unlike the majority of Wachau Riesling wines, those from the Salomon estate are bottled as late as September and always retain a 'spritz' of carbon dioxide. This makes for wines which are extremely appealing, fruity and elegant in their youth, but are also capable of long ageing.

FRANZ SCHMIDL

Weingut Franz Schmidl, 3601 Dürnstein 21

Estate bottled   4.5 acres of Riesling

12,000 bottles of Riesling per year

Quality: 🍇🍇🍇🍇   Price: ★★★ – ★★★★

Best vintages: '71, '73, '75, '79, '83, '86, '88

There is surely no baker anywhere in the world who is so talented a wine-maker as Franz Schmidl, or perhaps I should say that there is surely no other wine-maker anywhere in the world who is so talented a baker as Franz Schmidl. I doubt if bread can be more delicious than the Wachauer Laberl rolls which Franz Schmidl's bakery in Dürnstein produces. Simultaneously crispy and doughy, with a strong flavour from the dark flour used, they are the pinnacle of the Austrian baker's art. No wonder they are daily rushed by van to numerous towns in the surrounding area, and even to Vienna.

Though Franz Schmidl's wines are rather variable in quality, the best Rieslings he produces from his monopole Küss den

Pfennig (Kiss the Penny) site in Dürnstein are among the richest and most powerful dry Riesling wines in the Wachau. He also has a unique, completely subterranean, tasting room. It is a cold and dark, a cramped side gallery to the cellars which lie under his bakery in one of the narrow streets of medieval Dürnstein. Set into the wall are numerous pennies, which customers have been known to kiss at the end of tastings.

FREIE WEINGÄRTNER WACHAU

Freie Weingärtner Wachau, 3601 Dürnstein 107

168 acres of Riesling

540,000 bottles of Riesling per year

Quality: 🍇🍇🍇🍇 Price: ★★★ – ★★★★

Best vintages: '71, '77, '79, '82, '83, '86, '88

The Freie Weingärtner Wachau is probably the best co-operative winery in Europe. Wilhelm Schwengler directs it with the same commitment as he would if it were his own wine estate. In fact it is far more like a wine estate than a normal co-operative, all the vineyards originally having been the private estate of the von Kuenring family. In this form it is first recorded in 1137. When the von Kuenring family died out in 1355 the estate passed through the hands of numerous aristocratic families before, in 1938, the families who had long worked its vineyards jointly bought it. This created Austria's smallest wine co-operative, with just under 1,300 acres of vineyards.

The best wines from the Wachau co-op have always been good, but during the last decade Herr Schwengler has systematically improved the quality. In particular the Riesling wines of recent vintages from the great Achleiten site in Weissenkirchen have been as good as any other wines in the region. Like all the Wachau co-op's best wines they are made exclusively in wooden casks in their kilometre-long cellars deep under the vineyards of Dürnstein. All are very elegant, clean wines with an intense peachy fruit and crisp acidity.

CANADA

Total vineyard area: 22,500 acres

Vineyard area planted with Riesling: 2%/490 acres

Average annual Riesling production: 3,000,000 bottles

It is virtually unknown that Canada has a significant wine industry. The Canadian vineyards are concentrated in the east in Ontario on the shores of Lake Ontario and Lake Erie, and in the west in British Columbia in the Okanagan valley (see map, pp. 180–81). Wine, of sorts, has been produced in Ontario for many decades. However, until the late 1970s it was almost exclusively made from native and French–American hybrid vine varieties, as in New York State to the immediate south. It is only as a result of a handful of entrepreneurial owners of smaller wineries that wines from noble grape varieties are produced at all. Wine has been produced in the Okanagan valley only since the late 1940s, and it is only during the last decade that the noble vine varieties have been cultivated.

The most promising wine-growing area in Ontario is the Niagara Peninsula, sandwiched between Lake Ontario and Lake Erie, where the continental climate of inland North America is moderated by the influence of both lakes. Fine-wine production in the Okanagan valley, which lies 200 miles east of Vancouver, is also made possible by the moderating influence of deep lakes. None the less the climate in both areas is extreme compared with that of the classic European Riesling wine-growing regions, with very cold winters and hot summers. The Okanagan valley is also very arid, and irrigation is essential there. As a result of these extremes of temperature the white wines of both regions tend to be a little obvious. So far the Riesling wines of Ontario have been more successful than those of British Columbia. They have an extrovert exotic fruitiness and are fullish and juicy, with a softish acidity. Unfortunately the majority are made with a somewhat overbearing sweetness. The best come from the Inniskillin and Hillebrand estates, both in Niagara-on-the-Lake.

Given the youth of the fine-wine industry in Canada it is difficult to assess by how much wine producers there can improve on what has already been achieved. If for no other reason, Riesling has a firm future here because of its cold-resistance.

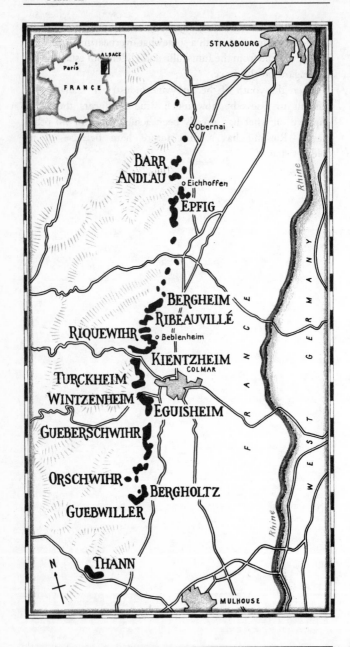

FRANCE

> Total vineyard area: 2,720,000 acres
>
> Vineyard area planted with Riesling: less than 1%/6,700 acres
>
> Average annual Riesling production: 30,000,000 bottles

It is perhaps strange that the Riesling vine has never established itself anywhere in France save in Alsace, since Champagne, Chablis, the Jura, and parts of the Loire valley possess a climate cool enough to produce high-class Riesling wines. The only Riesling vineyards in France outside Alsace are on an experimental scale.

Perhaps the reason the Riesling vine has never been popular in France as a whole is the difference in wine-making traditions between France and Germany. In France white wines tend to be quite high in alcohol (rarely below 11.5° and often above 13°) and to have rather soft acidity, and the best have some oak aromas and flavours from the new barrels in which they are matured. To a wine-maker who has made wines in this style all his life, a German Riesling invariably tastes thin, acidic, and lacking in precisely the special aromas and flavours which come from the typical French style of white wine-making. This impression is hardly going to persuade him to plant Riesling. With a new, much more open-minded and cosmopolitan generation entering the French wine industry perhaps this situation will change during the next decade.

Alsace

Total vineyard area: 31,500 acres

Vineyard area planted with Riesling: 21%/6,650 acres

Average annual Riesling production: 30,000,000 bottles

Alsace is a region with a unique character, steeped in both German and French traditions, yet also a world unto itself. Exactly the same could be said of its wine. Both the wine trade and consumers round the world have been taking an ever greater interest in the dry white wines of Alsace during recent years. Because they are quite soft and very aromatic, and therefore appealing from the moment they are released, the region is best known for its wines from the Gewürztraminer grape variety. While the greatest Gewürztraminer wines in the world are undoubtedly produced in Alsace, many of the top wine-growers in the region insist that their top Riesling wines outclass those from all the other regions' noble varieties. Outside the region this view is neither well known nor widely shared.

The reason that dry Alsace Riesling wines are not better known is undoubtedly their austerity. Drunk young, fine Alsace Rieslings tend to be rather firm and lean, with a reserved bouquet. After between three and five years' maturation in the bottle they blossom into wines which combine the concentration of a great white Burgundy with a sleek, cool elegance. Sadly, few people are lucky enough to have the opportunity to see what Alsace Riesling can become with bottle-maturation and to learn that they are wines which require patience.

The other problem is the enormous variation between the quality of the Riesling wines from the region's best vineyard sites and those from its poorest sites. Alsace lies further south than the great majority of the Riesling wine-growing regions of Germany, and one might think that it should therefore be easy to harvest grapes with the necessary ripeness to make good dry Riesling wines there. In the vineyards which lie on the well-exposed lower slopes of the Vosges mountains this is certainly the case, but many of the vineyards which lie on the plain are no better than the mediocre vineyards across the border in Germany's Rheinpfalz region. Riesling grapes ripen in such sites only in good vintages, and here the deep loamy soils make for high yields and rather thin, acidic wines. Wine-makers often try to obscure the unripeness with high alcohol levels, but the unripe flavours remain in the wines. Anyone looking for a modestly priced bottle from Alsace is strongly recommended to look for wines from the Pinot Blanc variety rather than to bother with the cheaper generic Rieslings.

The finest Alsace Riesling wines, however, are certainly among the world's greatest white wines. They owe their special character partly to the region's climate and partly to its wine-making traditions. The vineyards of Alsace lie in the rain shadow of the Vosges mountains, and rainfall is therefore low. Most importantly, the autumn in Alsace is so dry that the grapes can be left hanging in the vineyard until they reach full ripeness, without a serious risk of rot spoiling them. The generally clean state of the Riesling grapes harvested in Alsace enables the young wines to be left in contact with the 'lees' – the dead yeast which settles after fermentation – for a long time without the danger of unclean flavours developing. Through this extended lees contact the wines gain in aroma, extract, and 'fat'.

Top-quality Alsace Rieslings are consequently quite big wines, though their 11.5° to 12.5° of alcohol is comparatively modest compared with the 13° to 14° of white Burgundies. In addition to a considerable richness, they have a firm acidity and a strong minerally character. Like top German Riesling wines, fine Alsace Rieslings have a strong vineyard character. The huge variety of vineyard soils in Alsace makes for Riesling wines with radically different aromas and flavours. They can be peachy, pineappley, 'petrolly', flowery, herbal or vegetal, stony, or earthy according to the vineyard from which the grapes originated.

On 23 November 1983 the Alsace Grand Cru Appellation Contrôlée (AC) was introduced with twenty-five designated vineyard sites, to which a further twenty-two were added two years later. Each Grand Cru site is a precisely delimited area which must be a geological unity with a favoured aspect. Only wines from the four noble varieties (Riesling, Gewürztraminer, Tokay-Pinot Gris, and Muscat) can be sold as Grand Cru, and both a higher minimum level of ripeness and a lower maximum yield than for AC Alsace wines are required for a wine to be eligible. Finally there is a blind tasting in which the wine must demonstrate superior quality.

The Grand Cru system functions very well in guaranteeing a high quality level. It has also encouraged a new generation of dynamic, younger wine producers to work for the highest poss-ible quality. Although the 'Grandes Maisons', the larger wine houses, still play a very important role in the Alsace wine busi-ness, they are no longer the region's sole standard bearers.

The great majority of Alsace Riesling wines are dry, but during the last few years there has been an explosion in the production of rich late-harvested wines. There are two Appella-tions Contrôlées for wines in this style: Vendange Tardive (VT) and Sélection de Grains Nobles (SGN). The former may be dry or have a modest sweetness, but will always be full-bodied rich wines. The latter, made from grapes affected by noble rot (*Botrytis cinerea*), always have some sweetness and are lusciously rich. If dry Vendange Tardive Riesling wines can make an excellent accompaniment to roast game or to mature hard cheeses, Sélection de Grains Nobles Rieslings are dessert wines to be drunk either after a meal in place of dessert or with slightly sweet fruit desserts.

LUCIEN ALBRECHT

Lucien Albrecht, 68500 Orschwihr

Estate bottled

75 acres of Grand Cru Riesling

36 acres of other Riesling

20,000 bottles of Grand Cru Riesling per year

100,000 bottles of other Riesling per year

GRAND CRU PFINGTSBERG

Quality: 🍇🍇🍇🍇   Price: ★★★★★

OTHER RIESLINGS

Quality: 🍇🍇🍇   Price: ★★★

Best vintages: '71, '76, '83, '85, '88, '89, '90

Lucien Albrecht is one of the unknown wine-making talents of Alsace. Together with his son Jean he often makes better wines than some of his larger, much more renowned neighbours at the southern end of the Alsace vineyard. Of all the Albrechts' wines their Rieslings are the most consistent in quality. The Clos Himmelreich is an appealing, quite flowery wine, with enough forthright fruit to be enjoyed with food when quite young. The Riesling Cuvée Henri Albrecht is much more powerful and serious.

The Albrechts' Rieslings from the Grand Cru Pfingtsberg are big, concentrated, highly structured wines for laying down, needing a good five years' ageing in the bottle before they begin to show their full minerally complexity and mouthfilling peachy fruit. In 1983, '85, and '88 the Albrechts made superb late-harvested Vendange Tardive (VT) style Riesling wines from the Pfingtsberg. In contrast to the majority of Riesling VTs, they are completely dry wines with very firm acidity and incredibly concentrated fruit.

LEON BEYER

Leon Beyer, 68420 Eguisheim

5 acres of Riesling

180,000 bottles of Riesling per year

Quality: 🍇🍇🍇   Price: ★★★ – ★★★★

Best vintages: '71, '76, '79, '83, '85, '88, '89, '90

Tall, suave Marc Beyer runs one of the best wine-making houses in Alsace, producing wines of consistent elegance and harmony. For many years he has specialized in supplying the top restaurants of France, and there is hardly a restaurant in the country with a two- or three-star Michelin rating which does not list his wines. It is well worth tracking them down, for they are beautifully balanced, elegant and dry.

The Leon Beyer Riesling wines are made from a mix of grapes from vineyards owned by the company and grapes bought in from growers with whom the company has long-term contracts. Four grades of Riesling are produced. In order of ascending quality and richness they are Leon Beyer Riesling, Réservé, Cuvée des Écaillers, and Cuvée Particulière. The grapes for the last and most seldom produced of these *cuvées* usually come from Marc Beyer's own vineyards in the Pfersig-berg Grand Cru site, but this name never appears on the label. 'For the traditional *négociant* houses of Alsace the Grand Cru names don't make much sense,' Marc Beyer told me. 'We have to stick with the *cuvée* names which we've invested so much time and money in building up. They represent just as effective a guarantee of high quality for the consumer as they ever have.'

PAUL BLANCK

Paul Blanck, Domaines des Comtes de Lupfen, 68420 Kaysersberg

Estate bottled   20 acres of Riesling

50,000 bottles of Schlossberg Riesling per year

Quality: 🌳🌳🌳   Price: ★★★

Best vintages: '71, '76, '79, '83, '85, '88, '89, '90

'We make wines which come from the soil. If you have good vineyard sites such as we have you only have to choose the right moment to pick and make the wines carefully to achieve a high quality.' Such is the Blanck family's wine-making philosophy as expounded to me by one of its younger members, Philippe.

Stated this simply it somewhat belies the considerable trouble which the Blancks take to produce the best possible quality grapes in their vineyards in Kaysersberg, Sigolsheim, Ammerschwihr, Riquewihr, Colmar, and Saint Hippolyte. This is reflected most strongly in their Riesling wines, of which four are bottled with vineyard designations each vintage. The finest of these sites is undoubtedly the Grand Cru Schlossberg. Its weathered granite soil makes for wines of medium body, forthright fruit, and racy acidity. At the Blanck estate the wines have a particularly pronounced fruitiness as a result of being fermented in steel tanks.

Of their other Riesling wines those from the poor chalky soil of the Fürstentum, which gives wines with a creamy herbal character, are the most interesting. They tend to be most impressive in the 'average' vintages, as drought can be a problem here in a hot summer.

DOMAINES MARCEL DEISS

Domaines Marcel Deiss, 15 Route du Vin, 68750 Bergheim

Estate bottled

3 acres of Grand Cru Riesling

11 acres of other Riesling

6,000 bottles of Grand Cru Riesling per year

36,000 bottles of other Rieslings per year

Quality: 🍇🍇🍇🍇🍇   Price: ★★★ – ★★★★

Best vintages: '83, '85, '86, '87, '88, '89, '90

Jean-Michel Deiss is at once an extremely precise professional wine-maker and the wild man of Alsace. Shunned by many colleagues for his outspoken opinions, he has chosen to take his own, unconventional path. His shoulder-length slightly curly brown hair only accentuates the impression of wildness.

While many Alsace wine producers market their best wines under vineyard designations, Jean-Michel Deiss is perhaps the only one who markets all his Riesling wines under vineyard names. This is no marketing gimmick either, for each of the wines has an extremely distinct character.

Each vintage there are seven different bottlings of Riesling at the Deiss estate. The Riesling Saint Hippolyte from weathered granite soil is the simplest, though still an impressive wine, with pineappley fruit, medium body, and a piquant acidity. Of similar quality is the Riesling from the gravel soil of the Engelgarten site in Bergheim, which is racy and full of vibrant juicy fruit. The Riesling Burg from heavy marl soil in Bergheim is more powerful, with broad peachy fruit and a slight vegetal undertone. A truly unique wine is the Riesling from the Riesling Grasberg in Bergheim, where the grapes shrivel slightly on the vine before harvest owing to the dry calcareous soil, giving an intense citrusy-mango character.

A big jump up in concentration from these already excellent wines are the Riesling Grand Cru Altenberg from Bergheim and the Riesling Grand Cru Schoenenburg from Riquewihr. The Altenberg wines are really big mouthfuls even in so-called 'lesser' vintages, with a rich yet firm peachy fruit, plenty of extract and an almondy finish. The Schoenenburg Riesling wines are rich, packed with fruit, smoky, and earthy. These are among the very greatest dry Rieslings in Alsace.

DIRLER

Jean-Pierre Dirler, 13 rue de Issenheim, 68500 Bergholtz

Estate bottled   4.5 acres of Riesling

12,000 bottles of Riesling per year

Quality: 𝄞𝄞𝄞   Price: ★★★

Best vintages: '71, '76, '79, '81, '84, '85, '88, '89, '90

Jean-Pierre Dirler produces some of the cleanest and most refined Riesling wines in the southern part of Alsace. They have a crispness and raciness which are often reminiscent of the best Rieslings from the Rhine regions of Germany and are quite different from the majority of wines produced here, which often tend to be rather broad. As a result they make excellent food wines, matching fish, lobster, or meat dishes with a cream sauce particularly well.

Although Jean-Pierre's wines have the 12° of alcohol typical of Alsace Rieslings you wouldn't think so from the taste. Delicious drunk young, they age beautifully and can take more than five years' bottle ageing to reach their peak. In general the Dirler Riesling wines from Grand Cru Kesseler show the fullest fruit and the most aroma, but can be a little plump in the top vintages, while those from Grand Cru Spiegel and Saering are the most elegant.

DOPFF 'AU MOULIN'

Domaines Dopff 'Au Moulin', 68340 Riquewihr

Estate bottled   17.5 acres of Grand Cru Riesling

60,000 bottles of Grand Cru Riesling per year

Estate bottled   39.5 acres of other Riesling

120,000 bottles of other Rieslings per year

GRAND CRU RIESLINGS

Quality: 🍇🍇🍇🍇   Price: ★★★★

OTHER RIESLINGS

Quality: 🍇🍇🍇   Price: ★★★

Best vintages: '71, '76, '79, '81, '83, '85, '88, '89, '90

The house of Dopff 'Au Moulin', not to be confused with Riquewihr neighbours Dopff et Irion, are among the region's largest vineyard owners, possessing 185 acres of vineyards in the central part of Alsace. Together with the grapes they buy in from around 500 growers, this gives them an annual production of about 2,000,000 bottles of still wine and 600,000 bottles of Méthode Champenoise sparkling wine. It is the latter which the company is more famous for, Julien Dopff having pioneered sparkling wine production in the region during the early years of this century.

It is a tribute to Pierre-Étienne Dopff's direction of what remains a 100 per cent family-owned company that Dopff manage to make such a large quantity of modestly priced wines possessing good regional and varietal character, as well as a hundred thousand bottles per year of fine wines from their thirty-two acres of Grand Cru vineyards in Riquewihr and Turckheim. In order to differentiate clearly between the lighter wines made from bought-in grapes and the more intense wines made from their own vineyards, Dopff label the former with diamond-shaped labels and the latter with conventional rectangular labels.

Their finest Riesling is undoubtedly that from the Grand Cru Schoenenburg, which is late-harvested in good vintages and made in the rich Vendange Tardive (VT) style. These are full-bodied yet very elegant wines that need several years' maturation in the bottle before they show their best. They are slightly sweet, with concentrated peachy fruit and a touch of honey, and can mature for decades.

FALLER FRÈRE – DOMAINE WEINBACH

Mme Théo Faller et ses Filles, Domaine Weinbach, 68240 Kientzheim

Estate bottled   27.5 acres of Riesling

72,000 bottles of Riesling per year

Quality: 🍇🍇🍇🍇   Price: ★★★ – ★★★★

Best vintages: '71, '76, '82, '83, '85, '86, '88, '89, '90

Colette Faller is one of Alsace's top wine-makers. Her estate, situated between the villages of Kientzheim and Kaysersberg, was a convent until the French Revolution. It entered the ownership of her family in 1898, but it was only after the death of her husband Théo at the beginning of the eighties that the estate became famous.

The estate almost always harvests late, gathering grapes of each of the noble varieties at various levels of ripeness. To indicate the style and quality level of each of their wines, they have a rather complicated private classification system. The lowest grade of Riesling produced in most vintages is Réserve Particulière, which are rather steely medium-bodied wines.

The Riesling Cuvée de la Sainte Catherine wines, which are picked in November, have a wonderful combination of racy acidity and rich, ripe, even exotic fruit. They often have a little touch of sweetness too. They are followed by the full, honeyed Vendange Tardive dessert wines. These all originate from the Clos des Capuchins site which immediately surrounds the estate. Rather on one side from these wines is the Grand Cru Schlossberg Riesling, which makes up the larger part of the estate's Riesling wine production in most vintages. It is the best wine made from this site, with concentrated fruit and pronounced, yet elegant, acidity.

The atmosphere at Domaine Weinbach is quite unlike that of any other wine estate I've visited – at once serious and sophisticated, yet extremely relaxed. Colette Faller and her two daughters make everyone who visits feel at home, either in their parlour or round the kitchen table.

HUGEL

Hugel Père et Fils, 68340 Riquewihr

25.5 acres of Riesling

360,000 bottles of Riesling per year

VENDANGE TARDIVE AND SÉLECTION DES GRAINS
   NOBLES

Quality: 🥂🥂🥂🥂🥂   Price: ★★★★★
OTHER RIESLINGS

Quality: 🥂🥂🥂   Price: ★★★

Best vintages: '71, '76, '81, '83, '85, '88, '89, '90

The Hugel family are unquestionably the most famous wine producers in Alsace, and the region owes them a great debt for making the world aware that this beautiful region produces some of France's finest white wines. The great majority of Alsace's white wine production is dry, but the region's greatest wines are certainly the small quantities of dessert wines produced in the Vendange Tardive (VT) and Sélection des Grains Nobles (SGN) styles. These wine categories were in effect created by the Hugel family, who began making wines in this style a little over a century ago. As a result of the enormous experience which they have gained in their production, the law passed in April 1984 which governs the production of Alsace wines in these styles was virtually written by the Hugels.

There are probably no Rieslings anywhere in the world which can match the Hugel VT and SGN wines for sheer power. With between 12° and just over 13° of alcohol, a huge concentration of honeyed fruit, and firm acidity they are very big mouthfuls of wine. In the VT wines there is only the merest touch of sweetness, and they can be drunk either on their own, or with roasted game or semi-hard cheeses. The SGNs are much sweeter, but so rare that they should simply be savoured by themselves. Only six vintages of Hugel Riesling SGN have ever been produced: 1865, 1921, 1976, 1985, 1988 and 1989.

Étienne and Marc Hugel, the youngest generation of the family working in the business, are fanatics for these late-harvested wines. During the last few years they have made even more strenuous selections of botrytis-affected grapes in the vineyard in order to produce them. Their vineyard source is the Hugels' own vineyards in the Grand Cru Schoenenburg site, though this name will never appear on a Hugel label. It is also from here that the grapes for their top dry Riesling, Réserve Personnelle, usually come. This is by far the most interesting of their dry Rieslings, and is a full, earthy wine. The Hugels' simpler-quality Rieslings, made largely or wholly from bought-in grapes, are generally quite developed, soft and broad. They are easy to drink when they come onto the market, but can lack a little elegance.

*

KIENTZLER

André Kientzler, Route du Vin, 68150 Ribeauvillé
Estate bottled
4 acres of Grand Cru Riesling
10,000 of Grand Cru Riesling per year
VENDANGE TARDIVE AND SÉLECTION DES GRAINS
 NOBLES
Quality: 🍇🍇🍇🍇🍇   Price: ★★★★
OTHER RIESLINGS
Quality: 🍇🍇🍇🍇   Price: ★★★
Best vintages: '76, '79, '83, '85, '86, '88, '89, '90

André Kientzler is one of the most serious and thoughtful of the younger generation of Alsace wine-makers. Since the early eighties he has been producing some of the finest Riesling wines in the region in a singularly uninspiring modern building just to the north of Ribeauvillé. In particular, both his dry Rieslings from the Grand Cru Geisberg site and his Riesling Vendange Tardive and Sélection des Grains Nobles dessert wines are sensational.

André Kientzler has a very straightforward approach to wine-making. His wines are clean and elegant, yet also powerful and intense. Refreshingly for Alsace, they are never clumsy or alcoholic. 'I don't chaptalize much, because adding sugar to gain higher alcohol doesn't necessarily make the wine any better,' he told me. With such good vineyard sites as the Geisberg and Osterberg in Ribeauvillé, and very modest yields, André Kientzler harvests good, ripe grapes almost every vintage. He has also pioneered the production of Riesling ice wine (*vin de glace*) from frozen grapes harvested during December in Alsace.

★

MARC KREYDENWEISS

Marc Kreydenweiss, Domaine Fernand Gresser, 12 rue Deharbe, Andlau, 67140 Barr

Estate bottled   9 acres of Riesling

16,500 bottles of Riesling per year

Quality: 🍇🍇🍇🍇   Price: ★★★ – ★★★★

Best vintages: '71, '85, '86, '88, '90

Marc Kreydenweiss is a fanatical wine-grower. In a few short years he has made his wine estate in the little-known village of Andlau one of the top addresses for Riesling wines in the region. Through a sharp reduction in yields, and wine-making which mixes high tech and Heath Robinson, Marc Kreydenweiss has produced a string of magnificent Riesling wines from Andlau's two Grand Cru sites: Kastelberg and Wiebelsberg.

The most concentrated of these is undoubtedly that from the precipitously steep south-facing Kastelberg, whose weathered schist soil gives a wine which is very racy and minerally. Almost as fine, and much more accessible in their youth, are the richly fruity Rieslings from the south-west-facing Wiebelsberg. Here the red sandstone soil gives the wines a seductive juiciness and an almost opulently peachy bouquet.

Marc Kreydenweiss is obsessed with the fine differences of aroma and flavour which come from the soil, and his wine-making is dedicated to their intensification. To this end the vineyards are harvested in a series of selective pickings, and in the cellar the temperature of the fermenting wines is controlled by pumping water from the Andlau Bach, which flows directly past the cellar door through piping running through all the casks. The result is wines which are intense and finely nuanced.

GUSTAVE LORENTZ

> Gustave Lorentz, 68750 Bergheim
>
> 7 acres of Grand Cru Riesling
>
> 13 acres of Riesling
>
> 20,000 bottles of Altenberg Riesling per year
>
> 180,000 bottles of other Riesling per year
>
> Quality: 🍇🍇🍇   Price: ★★★
>
> Best vintages: '71, '76, '79, '83, '85, '86, '88, '89, '90

Georges Lorentz makes some of the best Riesling wines from the vineyards of Bergheim. Because of the heavy soils in this part of Alsace they are big, mouth-filling wines, with strong earthy bouquet. The most extreme examples of this very Alsatian style are the Rieslings from the Grand Cru Altenberg from Lorentz. They are broad, with an opulent apricoty-earthy fruit. Georges Lorentz's generic Riesling and Riesling Réserve are made from a mixture of grapes from his own vineyards around Bergheim and grapes bought from other growers in the area. Because of the relatively small area from which he buys grapes, these wines have a remarkably similar character to the Rieslings from the Altenberg.

JOS MEYER

> Jos Meyer et Fils, 76 rue de Clemenceau, 68000 Wintzenheim
>
> 7.5 acres of Grand Cru Riesling
>
> 24,000 bottles of Grand Cru Riesling per year
>
> Quality: 🍇🍇🍇   Price: ★★★
>
> Best vintages: '71, '76, '79, '83, '85, '88, '89

Jean Meyer makes a full, bold, unmistakably Alsace style of Riesling. Though his generic Riesling wines, largely made from bought-in grapes, are a little lean and simple, the better *cuvées* and Grand Cru wines are almost always impressive. The finer Riesling *cuvée*, Les Pierrets, has a wonderfully extrovert, flowery bouquet and full lush fruit on the palate. This is a wine for those who find most Alsace Rieslings too firm and acidic, since the softish acidity here is buried beneath considerable richness.

Of his estate-bottled Riesling wines the Grand Cru Hengst is clearly the best. It is a big, mouth-filling wine yet has a crisp enough acidity to prevent it from tasting heavy or over-blown. This is the kind of Riesling which can handle quite strong cheeses or light spicy meat dishes.

DOMAINE OSTERTAG

Domaine Ostertag, 87 rue Finkwiller, 67680 Epfig

4 acres of Grand Cru Riesling

7.5 acres of other Riesling

8,500 bottles of Grand Cru Riesling per year

20,000 bottles of other Rieslings per year

GRAND CRU MUENCHBERG RIESLING

Quality: 🍇🍇🍇🍇   Price: ★★★★

OTHER RIESLINGS

Quality: 🍇🍇   Price: ★★★

Best vintages: '83, '85, '86, '88, '89, '90

André Ostertag is perhaps the most original and dynamic of Alsace's young wine-makers, though whether his greater talent is as a wine-maker or as a self-publicist is a matter of some debate. Recently one of his more daring innovations, a Pinot Gris wine matured in new oak, was refused by the Alsace Appellation Contrôlée tasting commission. His classification of his own production into categories – Fruit Wines (whose character comes primarily from the varietal fruit of the grape), Stone Wines (whose character comes primarily from the soil of the vineyard), and Wood Wines (whose character is marked by maturation in new oak) – has been much derided by some of his colleagues.

There is no doubt in my mind that André Ostertag is a talented wine-maker though, and that his Riesling wines have come forward in leaps and bounds during the last five years. Perhaps the only thing that holds him back now is the quality of some of his vineyards. Epfig is situated somewhat to the east of the main body of the Alsace vineyard, and its vineyards are consequently more exposed. His simple Riesling d'Epfig is rather lean, tart, and appley. Much more accessible is the fuller, more fruity Riesling Heissenberg, which has a touch of exotic fruit in good vintages. The most severe of Ostertag's Rieslings is the steely, minerally Fronholtz, which can be very austere. Easily the best of the estate's Rieslings is the Grand Cru Muenchberg, which has a wealth of appley-white peach fruit. This is a wine which has enormous ageing potential, blossoming beautifully after between three and five years of maturation in the bottle.

DOMAINES SCHLUMBERGER

> Domaines Schlumberger, 100 rue Théodore-Deck, 68500 Guebwiller
>
> Estate bottled
>
> 60 acres of Grand Cru Riesling
>
> 120,000 bottles of Grand Cru Riesling per year
>
> Quality: 🍇🍇🍇🍇   Price: ★★★ – ★★★★
>
> Best vintages: '71, '76, '79, '83, '85, '88, '89

With nearly 350 acres of vineyards, Domaines Schlumberger are the largest vineyard owners in Alsace, with fully 1 per cent of the total vineyard area of the region in their possession. The heart of this is 190 acres in the Grand Cru sites of Guebwiller: Spiegel, Saering, Kessler, and the great Kitterle. From these sites Eric Beydon produces some highly impressive full-bodied dry Rieslings.

Schlumberger is one of the most traditional estates in Alsace, still working many of their vineyards by horse. For this reason the vineyards are terraced, and the vines are planted in rows running horizontally along the contours of the steep hillsides. The Schlumberger wines taste traditional too – big, broad, rich, and complex. The top Riesling wines are not released before they are two and a half years old and are often not bottled until the second summer after the harvest. Perhaps this is why some of the estate's wines seem just a shade blunt and heavy, as though the maturation process in cask and tank has sometimes gone just a little too far.

The minerally richness of the Schlumberger Rieslings, the product of low yields and late harvesting, makes them ideal for those who favour weight and power over delicacy. The finest of them, where elegance is added to the richness, are the Riesling wines from the Grand Cru Kitterle. They have a very full, almost chewy peachy fruit, with complex minerally aromas and a very long finish.

F. E. TRIMBACH

F. E. Trimbach, 68150 Ribeauvillé

3 acres of Riesling Clos Ste Hune

15.5 acres of Riesling

7,200 bottles of Riesling Clos Ste Hune per year

240,000 bottles of other Rieslings per year

RIESLING CLOS STE HUNE

Quality: 🍇🍇🍇🍇🍇   Price: ★★★★★

OTHER RIESLINGS

Quality: 🍇🍇🍇   Price: ★★★

Best vintages: '71, '75, '76, '79, '81, '83, '85, '86, '88, '89, '90

Of all the large wine-producing houses of Alsace, Trimbach has the most instantly recognizable wine style: crisp and very clean, with forthright fruit. They are also the most consistent of the larger Riesling producers, always making wines with elegance and charm. While their most direct competitors, Hugel, have made their name through late-harvested wines, Trimbach's top wine is a dry Riesling from their monopole Clos Ste Hune site.

Behind the half-timbered buildings which house the offices of F. E. Trimbach are the extensive cellars where Bernard and Pierre Trimbach make the wines, using a good deal of modern technology, though many of the top wines still ferment in wooden casks. The wines are filtered and bottled quite early compared with those of many other top producers in the region, and this is largely responsible for the house style. Even the simple Trimbach Riesling has a vivid, fruity, refreshing acidity and modest alcohol. The Riesling Réserve has quite a bit more depth and is only made in better vintages. Much more serious, firm and smoky, with concentrated fruit, is the Cuvée Frédéric Émile.

Easily the most powerful of the Trimbach Riesling wines is the Clos Ste Hune, which has been sold under this name since 1919. Modest yields, selective harvesting, the calcareous clay soil and warm micro-climate of the site makes for wines with extremely rich fruit. In the top vintages, subtle botrytis adds extra complexity and fat, but the acidity is always pronounced enough to balance. More than any other of the Trimbach wines, the Clos Ste Hune can mature in bottle for an extremely long time. In recognition of this the wine is only put onto the market when it is six years old.

DOMAINE ZIND-HUMBRECHT

Domaine Zind-Humbrecht, 34 rue du Maréchal Joffre, 68000 Colmar

Estate bottled

8.5 acres of Grand Cru Riesling

16.5 acres of other Rieslings

15,500 bottles of Grand Cru Rieslings per year

56,500 bottles of other Rieslings per year

Quality: ♟♟♟♟♟   Price: ★★★ – ★★★★★

Best vintages: '71, '76, '79, '83, '85, '86, '88, '89, '90

Ten years ago almost nobody had heard of Domaine Zind-Humbrecht. The estate was founded in 1959 when Leonard Humbrecht of Gueberschwihr married Ginette Zind of Wintzenheim. Throughout the sixties and seventies they progressively sold off their lesser, flat vineyards, and bought as much as they could afford of the excellent sites on the steep lower slopes of the Vosges mountains. With the good vintages of the early eighties this philosophy was vindicated. With a string of magnificent Riesling, Gewürztraminer, and Tokay wines Leonard was rapidly acclaimed one of the region's top wine-makers.

The dry Riesling wines from Zind-Humbrecht's Grand Cru sites Rangen and Brand are among the finest wines being made in this style anywhere in the world. Though Leonard Humbrecht and his son Olivier are master wine-makers they would both insist that without these top vineyards they would not be producing world-class Riesling wines. In the poor granite soil of the Brand just to the north-west of Turckheim, and the volcanic sediments of the Rangen above Thann right at the southern end of the region, the Riesling vines give an extremely low yield. In each case the wines' character is strongly influenced by the soil, the Brand Rieslings having an opulent pineappley fruit which leaps out of the glass at you, and the Rangen Rieslings very racy and minerally, with fine peachy fruit. The excellent micro-climates of these sites, particularly that of the precipitously steep Rangen, make for high levels of ripeness and richly fruity wines even in lesser vintages.

The wines from the non-Grand Cru Clos Heusen and Herrenweg sites are a little less intense and powerful, but beautifully balanced, elegant dry wines.

GERMANY

| Total vineyard area: 247,000 acres
| Vineyard area planted with Riesling: 20.5%/50,575 acres
| Average annual Riesling production: 240,000,000 bottles

Germany continues to produce more great Riesling wines than any other wine-growing nation in the world. However, this is not to say that everything is rosy in Germany's wine-producing regions. Many German wine producers are currently failing to realize the potential of their vineyards, and though the quality of dry German Riesling wines has greatly improved during the eighties, many of those from the Rheingau remain very unimpressive.

At their best German Riesling wines are very light in alcohol, generally having between 7.5° and 11°, and have as much intensity of aroma and flavour as the greatest white wines from other noble white-grape varieties. They are at the same time supremely elegant, very concentrated and complex, yet seductively fruity.

What gives the best German Riesling wines this exceptional elegance and finesse is a combination of climate, soil, and the nation's wine-making traditions. Whatever the New Zealanders would like to claim, Germany is *the* classic cool-climate viticultural region. The long ripening season and the large fluctuations between daytime and night-time temperatures are responsible for the filigree character of German Riesling wines. Even in great vintages, when there is a hot summer and autumn which results in super-ripe grapes and the wines are mouth-fillingly rich, they still taste sleek and racy. The further south you go in Germany the more this tart intensity is tempered and overlaid by an opulent ripe fruitiness.

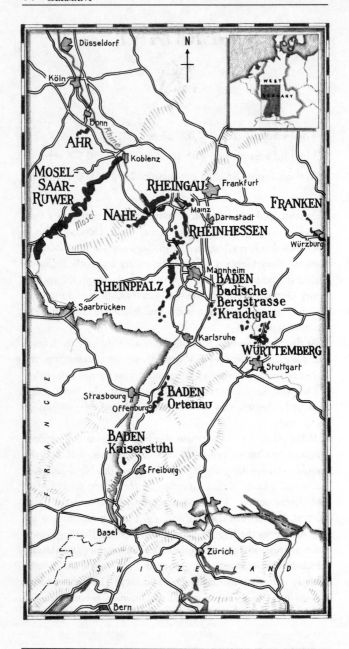

The stony and sandy soils of Germany's top vineyard sites also contribute to the many-layered complexity of the wines' aroma and flavour. The better a German Riesling wine is the more pronounced the character from the vineyard will be. Unfortunately, the fashion in Germany during the last decade has been for very clean, neutral Riesling wines, and this hasn't encouraged wine producers to make wines with a pronounced character. This is now beginning to change, and a new generation is reducing yields and altering wine-making techniques in order to make wines with more vineyard character and greater individuality. The top producers of Germany all bottle their best wines barrel by barrel, and it is quite normal for them to produce bottlings of less than a hundred cases.

German wine-making has always emphasized primary flavours and aromas – the flavours and aromas which come from the grapes rather than from wine-making. Many German wine-makers would go so far as to say that their wines should have precisely the same flavours as the grapes from which they were made. Others look for some secondary characteristics, from contact of the wine with the yeast after fermentation or maturation in old oak barrels. Whichever style of wine-making is used, intense fruit, and a balance of this with the wine's natural acidity and extract, are the grower's aim.

The other component in this delicate balancing act, sweetness, has become the subject of some controversy during recent years. Certainly the majority of Germany's wines before the last world war were dry, and the rediscovery of this dry wine-making tradition during the last decades has been an important learning process for German wine-makers. Undeniably many German Riesling wines produced in the sixties and seventies were too sweet, and the rejection of this style is to be welcomed. However, in my view most of the bone-dry (Trocken) Riesling wines from the Mosel–Saar–Ruwer, Nahe, and Rheingau are too acidic. Thankfully the move in these regions is towards harmoniously dry wines (the Charta wines from the Rheingau, for example), or traditional-style wines with a much reduced sweetness.

The political developments in East Germany during 1989

focused attention on everything East German, including the country's wine production. The 1,500 acres of East German vineyards are mostly situated on south-facing slopes in the Saale–Unstrut area and in the valley of the Elbe south-east of Dresden. They lie considerably further north than the classic West German wine-producing region. Unfortunately, the Riesling wines from East Germany are awful. Bone-dry and alcoholic, with a harsh acidity, they are *not* recommended. Better wines are made from other white-wine varieties such as Müller-Thurgau and Weissburgunder (Pinot Blanc).

Baden

Total vineyard area: 37,000 acres

Vineyard area planted with Riesling: 7.5%/2,750 acres

Average annual Riesling production: 10,000,000 bottles

Baden is Germany's warmest wine-growing region, and the only one to be placed in climatic category B of the EEC's regional classification for viticulture (along with Champagne and the Loire). Its wine-growing traditions are rather different from those of the Rhine or Mosel regions though, and Riesling plays an important role in only two corners of the region. However, during the last twenty years its Riesling acreage has more than doubled, and at least some Riesling is to be found in all its sub-areas, which stretch from round Heidelberg in the north down to Meersburg on Lake Constance in the south.

There can be little doubt though that the Baden Riesling wines most deserving of international attention are those from Ortenau and Kaiserstuhl. The Ortenau is a long strip of vineyards which cover the lower slopes of the northern end of the Black Forest, and the best sites for Riesling lie on granitic hills immediately to the east of the town of Offenburg. Though

Riesling usually tends to prefer a cool climate, the other area of
Baden where it has long been established as an important grape
variety is far to the south on the slopes of the Kaiserstuhl. The
Kaiserstuhl is the stump of an extinct volcano, and its southern
and western slopes have an exceptionally warm, dry climate.

In comparison to the top Alsace Rieslings, Baden Rieslings
tend to lack a little real power, but on the plus side they are less
alcoholic. Baden undoubtedly has the best chance of establishing a good international reputation for itself with its dry Weiss-
burgunder (Pinot Blanc) and Grauburgunder (Pinot Gris)
wines, but its dry Rieslings are far more than mere curiosities.

FREIHERR FRANCKENSTEIN

Ortenau

Weingut Freiherr von & zu Franckenstein, Wein-
  gartenstrasse 66, 7600 Offenburg

12 acres of Riesling

40,000 bottles of Riesling per year

Quality: 🍇🍇🍇🍇   Price: ★★★ – ★★★★

Best vintages: '79, '83, '86, '88, '89, '90

Possibly because of his rather serious introverted manner, or
possibly because of the bizarre name of his estate, Hubert Doll
has so far failed to make much of a reputation for his excellent
dry Riesling wines even within Germany. Brimming with peach
and pineapple fruit, richly aromatic, yet crisp and elegant, they
are textbook examples of Ortenau white wines. Even in lesser
vintages these are some of the finest dry Riesling wines in the
country.

In spite of its aristocratic name, which was the inspiration for
the title of Mary Shelley's novel, the estate's buildings are
drearily practical. Looking much like any number of other large
houses on the outskirts of Offenburg, there is nothing to mark
them out as the source of some of Baden's best white wines.

DR HEGER

Kaiserstuhl

Weingut Dr Heger, Bachenstrasse 19–20, 7811 Ihringen

Estate bottled   5.5 acres of Riesling

15,000 bottles of Riesling per year

Quality: 🍇🍇🍇   Price: ★★★

Best vintages: '79, '81, '83, '86, '88, '89, '90

Joachim Heger makes the most elegant dry Rieslings in southern Baden. They come from the great Ihringer Winklerberg site, which has the warmest micro-climate of any vineyard in Germany. From this site, which was created out of rocky scrub at the beginning of the last century, remarkably crisp, minerally, dry Riesling wines can be produced considering the warm climate. This is due to the vineyard's extremely stony soil, which is the product of the weathering of the volcanic cliffs which lie behind its precipitous slopes.

Nobody who visits the Dr Heger estate could fail to be impressed by Joachim Heger's passion for wine. Considering the estate's remarkable success as an important supplier to dozens of Germany's top restaurants and merchants, everything at the Dr Heger estate is extremely relaxed and open. The only stage at which there is no relaxation is in the making of the wines. Joachim tastes the young wines every day from cask, where they lie together on the yeast lees for as long as possible. This technique gives the Dr Heger Riesling wines a very intense fruitiness to balance their racy acidity.

Franken

Total vineyard area: 13,300 acres

Vineyard area planted with Riesling: 3%/385 acres

Average annual Riesling production: 3,250,000 bottles

In the vineyards of Franken, or Franconia as it is usually called in the English-speaking world, the Riesling vine is a rarity. The region's vineyards are dominated by the Müller-Thurgau and Silvaner varieties, and a wide selection of new vine crossings (of dubious merit). However, the small acreage of Riesling is concentrated in the hands of a few top estates which make high-class dry white wines. Though there is only space to report on two producers in Franken this suffices to give a fairly complete picture of quality Riesling production in the region.

Franken's dry Riesling wines are strongly marked by the region's relatively continental climate and by the heavy limestone and marl soils in its vineyards. They are broad, but the best are not too heavy, having a firm earthy flavour and a big aftertaste.

Franken wines are instantly recognizable on the shelf, for they are invariably filled in flagon-shaped bottles called '*Bocksbeutel*', which means 'goat's scrotum' – not an appetizing idea, but they are excellent food wines that can stand up to strongly flavoured meat or river fish dishes.

BÜRGERSPITAL

> Bürgerspital zum Heiligen Geist, Theaterstrasse 19, 8700 Würzburg
>
> Estate bottled   61.5 acres of Riesling
>
> 240,000 bottles of Riesling per year
>
> Quality: 🍇🍇🍇🍇   Price: ★★★ – ★★★★
>
> Best vintages: '71, '76, '79, '83, '85, '88, '90

The Bürgerspital foundation, founded in 1319 in the historic city of Würzburg, is one of the oldest, largest wine estates in Germany, and the finest producer of Riesling wines from the great Stein vineyard to the north of the city. The wines from this site used to be renowned for their smokiness, but this may have had more to do with the fact that the main railway line runs along the foot of the vineyard, the grapes bringing some soot with them into the cellars. Today the Bürgerspital's wines from the Stein taste *clean* and firm, with a mouth-filling fruit and a subtle earthiness.

If care isn't taken in the cellar to preserve their freshness, the wines from the vineyards along the Main river valley in Franken, with their heavy limestone soils, can be rather flat and lifeless, dominated by alcohol. Of all the estates in this, the larger sub-area of the region, the Bürgerspital most successfully produces wines which have elegance as well as body and substance.

HANS WIRSCHING

Weingut Hans Wirsching, Ludwigstrasse 16, 8715 Iphofen

Estate bottled   13.5 acres of Riesling

46,000 bottles of Riesling per year

Quality: 🍇🍇🍇   Price: ★★★ – ★★★★

Best vintages: '71, '75, '76, '79, '83, 85, '88, '90

The Wirsching estate is run by Dr Heinrich Wirsching, who make extremely clean, fruity dry Riesling wines. His estate, whose history goes back over 350 years, is situated in the Steigerwald area of Franken on the western flank of the region. Here the soils are mostly of heavy gypsum marl and the climate yet more extreme than that of Würzburg at the region's centre.

The Wirsching's finest Riesling wines come from the Iphofer Julius-Echter-Berg, probably the best vineyard site in the entire Steigerwald. They have body, concentration, elegance, and an excellent inner harmony. Those which are not dry (for instance the rare Auslese wines) have naturally retained the hint of sweetness they possess.

Mosel–Saar–Ruwer

Total vineyard area: 31,500 acres

Vineyard area planted with Riesling: 56%/17,500 acres

Average annual Riesling production: 80,000,000 bottles

The valleys of the Mosel, and its tributaries the Saar and Ruwer, are famous for producing Riesling wines of the greatest delicacy and elegance. The Riesling vine has been grown here for more than five hundred years, and for almost two centuries the Riesling wines from the precipitously steep vineyards of this northerly region have been renowned for their flowery bouquet, vividly fruity, racy flavour, and lightness of body.

Unfortunately, during the last twenty-five years large areas of new vineyards have been planted with new vine crossings on flat ground round the steep traditional vineyard sites. These new plantations of inferior varieties give enormous yields of thin, watery, sweetish wine. This sugar-water, sold for low prices under the names Piesporter Michelsberg, Bereich Bernkastel, Bernkasteler Kurfürstlay, and Ürziger Schwarzlay, did much to spoil the region's good name during this period.

There has also been a tendency for some Riesling producers to make their wines too sweet, smothering the finely nuanced fruit character which makes them unique. In spite of containing some unfermented sweetness, a well-made Mosel–Saar–Ruwer Riesling of Qualitätswein or Kabinett quality should never taste sweet.

Thankfully a large number of the region's estates are today producing elegant traditional-style wines with a restrained touch of sweetness, as well as ever more harmonious dry (Trocken and Halbtrocken) wines. The name Riesling plus that of any of the producers recommended here is an effective guarantee of high-quality Mosel wine. Indeed, the Mosel–Saar–Ruwer produces more really top-quality Riesling wines than any other region in Germany. In the lightly sweet and dessert-wine styles they are the finest Riesling wines in the world.

The move towards more balanced wines during the last decade has made the special character of the region's wines, and of the individual vineyards, much more apparent than it was in the past. The reduction of yields by some of the dynamic wine-makers in the younger generation has further accentuated this. The most typical aroma of fine Mosel Riesling wines is the piquant minerally tone which they gain from the extremely stony slate soils.

The most important variations within the Riesling wines of the region are between those of the Lower Mosel, the Middle Mosel, the Ruwer valley and the Saar valley. The fullest bodied are the wines of the Lower Mosel. In lesser vintages they can be rather angular, but are sleek and elegant in good and top vinta-ges. Middle Mosel Riesling wines are more flowery, forth-rightly fruity, and filigree. In the really top vintages they are rich and succulently fruity, but never heavy. They have an elegant acidity, and the best are extremely long-lived. Ruwer wines of lesser vintages are tart and piquant, while in better vintages they combine richness with a remarkable delicacy and a subtle flowery bouquet. Saar wines show the greatest variation between poor and top vintages. In years not blessed with much sun they are often aggressively acidic. This same firm structure gives them a sensational brilliance in great vintages, often unmatched in the whole of Germany.

Though many wine-makers in the region also have some stainless-steel or fibreglass tanks in their cellars, the majority of the region's Riesling wines continue to be made in wooden casks. Roman remains suggest that the wooden casks used to transport the wines during the third century AD were of the same form and capacity as those used today. Because of the delicacy of Mosel Riesling wines these casks are treated before use so that they don't give the wines an obvious oaky taste, which would spoil their delicate flavour and bouquet.

Kabinett-quality Riesling wines from the Mosel–Saar–Ruwer are among the world's lightest wines, containing between 7° and 8.5° of alcohol and an exceptionally refreshing lively fruiti-ness. There could be no better wine to drink as an aperitif or simply while relaxing with friends. The richer, late-harvested

Riesling Spätlese and Auslese wines barely have any more alcohol, though they taste far fuller and more concentrated.

JOH. JOS. CHRISTOFFEL

Mosel

Schanzstrasse 2, 5564 Ürzig

Estate bottled   5.5 acres of Riesling

22,000 bottles of Riesling per year

Quality: 🍇🍇🍇🍇   Price: ★★★

Best vintages: '71, '75, '76, '79, '83, '85, '88, '90

The quiet perfectionism of Hans Leo Christoffel has ensured that his small estate has remained one of the undiscovered star Riesling producers of the Mosel. His beautifully restored 300-year-old house tucked in among the narrow backstreets of Ürzig can only be found by those who actively seek it.

The Riesling wines from the great Ürziger Würzgarten and Erdener Treppchen sites are among the richest and spiciest in the entire Mosel–Saar–Ruwer. Often they can be full to the point of plumpness. However, those from Joh. Jos. Christoffel match the spicy, exotic richness so characteristic of Ürzig and Erden with a remarkable elegance.

The other remarkable characteristic of the Joh. Jos. Christoffel wines is that they are shockingly cheap for the quality. There can hardly be any better value in Riesling wines anywhere in the world.

FRITZ HAAG

Middle Mosel

Dusemonder Hof, 5551 Brauneberg

Estate bottled   13 acres of Riesling

50,000 bottles of Riesling per year

Quality: 🍇🍇🍇🍇🍇   Price: ★★★ – ★★★★★

Best vintages: '71, '75, '76, '79, '83, '85, '88, '89, '90

Nobody who has met Wilhelm Haag can doubt his unswerving commitment to producing wines of the highest quality. His energy and enthusiasm are those of a man a full generation younger than his fifty-four years. You also find this energy in his wines, which are very concentrated and highly structured. They are not for anyone seeking a pleasant uncomplicated wine though. Even his simple quality (QbA) wines which he markets simply as Fritz Haag Riesling have a wonderful vibrancy and intensity of fruit.

To look at the Fritz Haag estate house, a pleasant if unexceptional example of 1960s domestic architecture, you would never imagine that such wines could be made here. Very few people get to see the equally unremarkable concrete barrel cellar which lies below the rustic reception rooms of Wilhelm Haag's house. 'I am solely responsible for what happens in here, I taste the young wines as often as possible from the barrel, and only do what is absolutely necessary to them,' is as much as Wilhelm Haag reveals about his wine-making, though it is half the secret of his superb wines. The view from the terrace in front of the estate across the Mosel to the precipitous slopes of the 'Grand Cru' Brauneberger Juffer and Juffer-Sonnenuhr vineyards tells you the other half of the secret.

The richness and subtle earthiness of the Brauneberg Rieslings enables Wilhelm Haag regularly to make dry Riesling wines harmonious enough to appeal to non-German palates. Although most of these are consumed within Germany, some are also exported. The Haag Riesling wines in the traditional style have an exceptional ageing capacity, and show an impress-

ive weight and complexity when they reach their peak after five
to twenty years in the bottle.

REINHOLD HAART

Middle Mosel

Weingut Reinhold Haart, Ausoniusufer 18, 5555 Piesport

Estate bottled   10 acres of Riesling

50,000 bottles of Riesling per year

Quality: 🍇🍇🍇🍇   Price: ★★★ – ★★★★

Best vintages: '71, '75, '76, '79, '83, '88, '89, '90

Because of the strength of demand for its wines from Japan, and
the reputation of Piesport for cheap bulk wines in the English-
speaking world, the name of the great Piesporter Goldtröpfchen vineyard site is too little known internationally. The Piesporter Goldtröpfchen doesn't just have a romantic name, it also
has some of the finest south-facing slopes on the entire length
of the Mosel. Sitting in the crook of one of the river's enormous
loops, the vines are almost completely protected from cold
winds. This, combined with the deep slaty soils, give the Piesport wines a special character. In good or top vintages they are
rich, but never heavy, having a tartness and slight anise touch
which perfectly set off the intense ripe fruit flavours.

Of the many small producers in Piesport, the Reinhold Haart
estate is clearly the best. Owner and wine-maker Theo Haart is
a quietly spoken man, but possessed of strong views. Although
he has no problem selling his entire production for good prices
he considers the crude commercialization of the good name of
Piesport for the marketing of wines from the inferior vineyards
of other villages 'a disaster for us and for wine drinkers in many
countries who are being misled in a manner which the present
law encourages'. His wines are packed with fruit, extremely
elegant, and never too sweet.

VON HÖVEL

Saar

> Weingut von Hövel, Agritiusstrasse 5–6, 5501 Konz–
> Oberemmel
>
> Estate bottled   29 acres of Riesling
>
> 125,000 bottles of Riesling per year
>
> Quality: ♥♥♥♥   Price: ★★ – ★★★★
>
> Best vintages: '71, '75, '76, '79, '82, '83, '85, '88, '89

If you met Eberhart von Kunow only briefly you would find it hard to believe that he is one of the top wine producers of the Mosel–Saar–Ruwer. How does someone who seems to make a joke of wine and everything else produce such good wines? The von Hövel Rieslings may lack the richness of Egon Müller's top wines or the steely intensity of Zilliken's, but the best make up for this with sheer fruit and verve.

A Riesling Kabinett from von Hövel's monopole vineyard site Oberemmeler Hütte is the ideal introduction to Saar Riesling, a touch of sweetness perfectly setting off the elegant acidity to give a lively piquant fruitiness. These wines aren't dry, nor could they be called sweet, but they are extremely clean and refreshing in flavour. The Hütte also gives fine Spätlese wines which are extremely elegant and long in flavour. The von Hövel wines from the Schwarzhofberg are much fuller and weightier.

IMMICH-BATTERIEBERG

Middle Mosel

> Weingut Carl. Aug. Immich-Batterieberg, 5585 Enkirch
>
> Estate bottled   15 acres of Riesling
>
> 55,000 bottles of Riesling per year
>
> Quality: ♥♥♥♥   Price: ★★★ – ★★★★
>
> Best vintages: '71, '75, '76, '79, '81, '82, '85, '88, '89, '90

Georg Immich's wines are deliberately old-fashioned in style. They are so different from the majority of Mosel Rieslings that they split even professional tasters into two opposing camps. A visit to the Immich-Batterieberg estate explains much about the wines' character. The buildings themselves give a distinctly medieval impression. Yields are low, and the harvest is very late, making for rich, powerful wines. The grapes are pressed in hydraulic basket presses of the kind which today are normally to be found only in museums, and the wines are fermented and matured exclusively in wooden casks. There has never been a time when over-sweetened wines have been produced here, and even the Immich-Batterieberg Auslese wines taste off-dry.

All the estate's wines come from vineyards in Enkirch. The finest are almost invariably the Spätlese and Auslese from the Enkircher Batterieberg (no wines of lesser-quality grades are marketed under this name). This site was created by one of Georg Immich's ancestors in the 1840s by dynamiting the cliffs which previously occupied this steep craggy hillside. The Batterieberg wines are powerful, minerally, and complex. They have an extremely long life and don't show their full character until they have been in the bottle for at least five years.

KARLSMÜHLE

Ruwer

Weingut Karlsmühle, 5501 Mertesdorf

Estate bottled   16 acres of Riesling

66,000 bottles of Riesling per year

Quality: 🍇🍇🍇🍇   Price: ★★★ – ★★★★

Best vintages: '71, '75, '76, '86, '88, '89, '90

Peter Geiben's vineyards, which make up the monopole Mertesdorfer Lorenzhof site, lie immediately behind his charming Karlsmühle hotel. The hotel took up the greater part of the Geiben family's interests and attention until recently.

However, since Peter Geiben took over the wine-making at the Karlsmühle estate in the mid-eighties it has become one of the leading producers in the Ruwer valley. The wines are very racy and intense, and as much effort is put into the production of rich Auslese and Beerenauslese dessert wines as into dry-wine production. This is surely a great estate in the making!

KARTHÄUSERHOF/TYRELL

Ruwer

Rautenstrausch'sche   Weingutsverwaltung   Karthäuserhof, Karthäuserhof, 5500 Trier–Eitelsbach

Estate bottled   40 acres of Riesling

130,000 bottles of Riesling per year

Quality: ♕♕♕♕   Price: ★★★ – ★★★★★

Best vintages: '71, '73, '75, '86, '88, '89, '90

The way in which Christoph Tyrell has turned the fortunes of the Karthäuserhof estate round during the last five years is truly remarkable. In 1985, when his father, Werner Tyrell, stood trial for having illegally added sugar to many of the estate's best wines (the law against which he had helped write!), it looked as if the estate might have to be sold off. However, Christoph Tyrell came to the rescue, giving up his law practice in Trier to run the estate, which he officially took control of in the spring of 1987. He changed the style of the wines to make them fresher and more vividly fruity than in the past, and dramatically increased the proportion of dry wines.

Anyone who thinks that German Riesling wines are to be drunk only on their own should try one of Christoph Tyrell's drier-style wines as he would serve it, with game. Many wine estate owners in the Mosel–Saar–Ruwer are avid hunters, and none more so than Christoph Tyrell. Wild duck and dry Karthäuserhofberg Riesling is a wonderful combination and often comes to the table at Karthäuserhof. Though light in alcohol,

Christoph Tyrell's wines have more than enough steely intensity to stand up to the strong flavours of the game.

HERIBERT KERPEN

Middle Mosel

> Weingut Heribert Kerpen, Hauptstrasse 77 & Uferallee 6,
> 5550 Bernkastel–Wehlen
>
> Estate bottled   6 acres of Riesling
>
> 35,000 bottles of Riesling per year
>
> Quality: 🍇🍇🍇   Price: ★★★ – ★★★★
>
> Best vintages: '71, '75, '76, '83, '85, '88, '90

Since the death of her husband, whose name the estate bears, in 1963 Hanne Kerpen has run this fine small estate in Wehlen with the help of her three sons. For many years the wines were made under difficult conditions in a number of small cellars scattered round the village of Wehlen. In 1986 Hanne Kerpen and her youngest son, Martin, bought an imposing old house on the Uferallee and finally brought all their wine-making under one roof.

To look at the cellars of the estate, with their nineteenth-century basket press and narrow galleries filled with wooden casks, you would think that its wines might be rather rustic, but the opposite is the case. Martin Kerpen makes very clean, 'spritzy' wines with a subtly nuanced fragrance. The one possible criticism of them is that they are sometimes a little too light and too sweet, lacking power on the finish.

REICHSGRAF VON KESSELSTATT

Mosel, Saar, and Ruwer

> Liebfrauenstrasse 10, 5500 Trier
>
> Estate bottled   166.5 acres of Riesling

650,000 bottles of Riesling per year

Quality: 🍷🍷🍷🍷   Price: ★★★ – ★★★★★

Best vintages: '71, '75, '79, '83, '85, '88, '89, '90

For several years the Kesselstatt estate has produced the best wines of all the large Trier-based estates. With its new cellars below Schloss Marienlay in the Ruwer valley, the consistency of the wines has been greatly improved, and there can now be no doubt that Kesselstatt is the best of the large estates in the Mosel–Saar–Ruwer region.

What makes this particularly remarkable is that owner Günther Reh is also the owner of a company (Faber) producing huge quantities of cheap sparkling wines, and of a number of other wine businesses on the Mosel which also concentrate on the lower price bracket. He leaves the running of the estate in the competent hands of his eldest daughter, Annegret Reh-Gartner, who has done an impressive job in rationalizing the estate and building up its reputation internationally.

The Kesselstatt vineyards are scattered extremely widely, the largest single plot being the fifteen acres of the Josephshöfer in Graach, a vineyard site solely owned by the estate. This gives full, firm, earthy wines, which in top vintages have an impressive richness and enough structure to age for decades. Impressive Mosel Rieslings are also made from the estate's substantial vineyard holdings in Piesport. On the Saar, Kesselstatt own eleven acres of the famous Scharzhofberg. However, the wines from their vineyards at Kasel on the Ruwer have been among the best from the estate in recent vintages.

DR LOOSEN

Middle Mosel

St Johannishof, 5550 Bernkastel

Estate bottled   18.5 acres of Riesling

45,000 bottles of Riesling per year

ERDENER PRÄLAT RIESLING

Quality: 🍷🍷🍷🍷🍷   Price: ★★★★

OTHER RIESLINGS

Quality: 🍷🍷🍷🍷   Price: ★★★

Best vintages: '71, '75, '76, '85, '88, '89, '90

Until Ernst Loosen took over the Dr Loosen estate in January 1988 it was only in the very best vintages that the estate made good wines. Since then it has belonged to the small group of elite estates in the region, producing wines of richness, elegance, and complexity. Ernst Loosen never planned to run the family estate, and it was only his father's ill health in 1983 which brought him back from the University of Mainz, where he was studying archaeology. With the appointment of cellar master Bernhard Schug in 1987 the estate started achieving the full potential of its excellent vineyards in the Erdener Treppchen and Prälat, Ürziger Würzgarten, Wehlener Sonnenuhr, Graacher Himmelreich, and Bernkasteler Lay.

Ernst Loosen and Bernhard Schug's wine-making is a return to the techniques normal before the age of high technology. In the vineyards they have radically cut the yields by abandoning chemical fertilizers, by harder pruning, and by selective harvesting. 'We want to make wines with as much weight and depth as possible,' Ernst Loosen explains, 'wines with a very clear vineyard character.'

The wines with the strongest, and most individual, vineyard character are those from the Erdener Prälat, a very small site sandwiched between massive red slate and sandstone cliffs and the river. Its optimal micro-climate and special soil (also red slate and sandstone) give wines with a luscious fruitiness, and characteristic flavours are of bitter almonds.

MAXIMIN GRÜNHAUS/C. VON SCHUBERT

Ruwer

C. von Schubert'sche Gutsverwaltung, 5501 Grünhaus

Estate bottled   74 acres of Riesling

240,000 bottles of Riesling per year

Quality: 🍷🍷🍷🍷🍷   Price: ★★★ – ★★★★★

Best vintages: '71, '73, '75, '76, '79, '83, '85, '88, '89, '90

Of the larger wine estates in the Mosel–Saar–Ruwer region there can be little doubt that Maximin Grünhaus consistently makes the best-quality wines. Carl von Schubert's wines are the finest expression of the special character of Rieslings from the little Ruwer valley near the city of Trier. Even the simple quality (QbA) wines have an extremely fine bouquet of flowers, herbs, and 'slate' from the soil. In the late-harvested wines this is filled out with a fine appley or peachy fruit, and sometimes a hint of honey from botrytis. However rich these wines are they always retain a delicacy, such that fruit and acidity seem balanced on the point of a pin.

Carl von Schubert is one of very few wine producers in Germany lucky to have all his vineyards together in one block close to the estate buildings, like those of a Bordeaux *château*. The estate is divided into three vineyard sites, Abtsberg, Herrenberg, and Bruderberg, all of which it owns exclusively.

Carl von Schubert is a very strong believer in preserving the classic style of the wines of the region, and of his own estate. While he has refined many details of the wine-making at Maximin Grünhaus since taking the estate over from his father, Andreas von Schubert, in 1981, the wine style hasn't changed. The large proportion of the Maximin Grünhaus wines, fully two thirds of the production, which are made in the dry style (Trocken), and the modest amount of sweetness in the conventional-style wines, are consequences of this conservatism. The great majority of the wines are allowed to decide for themselves whether they will be dry or retain some sweetness. The dry wines are among the very best in the region, having an abundance of fruit and an excellent harmony. In spite of their delicacy the Maximin Grünhaus wines have the potential to age for a very long time. Kabinett wines can still be fresh at ten or more years of age, and higher qualities can age even longer.

EGON MÜLLER-SCHARZHOF

Saar

Scharzhof, 5511 Wiltingen

Estate bottled   20 acres of Riesling

80,000 bottles of Riesling per year

RIESLING AUSLESE, BEERENAUSLESE, TROCKENBEEREN-
AUSLESE, EISWEIN

Quality: 🍇🍇🍇🍇🍇   Price: ★★★★★

OTHER RIESLINGS

Quality: 🍇🍇🍇   Price: ★★★★

Best vintages: '71, '75, '76, '79, '83, '85, '88, '89, '90

The Egon Müller estate is renowned for producing Germany's most expensive wines, the best 1989 Riesling Auslese having sold for DM 298 per bottle at auction in September 1990, and the 1983 Riesling Eiswein for DM 1,280 at auction in October 1984 – the highest price ever paid for a young white wine. While it says much for the sophisticated salesmanship of Egon Müller Snr that he has reached a price level which most other German wine producers can only dream of, this could never have been achieved without the succession of remarkable late-harvested Riesling wines which the Müller estate has produced since the late forties. In virtually every one of the area's good or top vintages, the top wines of the Egon Müller estate stand out as the best. Egon Müller's Scharzhofberger Auslese, Beerenauslese, Trockenbeerenauslese, and Eiswein have a combination of honeyed richness and refinement that is totally seductive.

A tasting of young wines at the Egon Müller estate early in the year can be anything but seductive though. The wines stand in a circle on a small marble table in the icy entrance hallway, and both Egon Müller Snr and Jr stand to one side waiting quietly and patiently. The cold together with the somewhat raw youthfulness of the wines at this time makes it a severe experience until you reach the last glasses on the table and the honeyed richness of the vintage's best wines. This combination of severity and lusciousness seems to say everything about the wines of this region and of the Egon Müller estate in particular.

JOH. JOS. PRÜM

Middle Mosel

Uferallee 19, 5550 Bernkastel–Wehlen

Estate bottled   34.5 acres of Riesling

130,000 bottles of Riesling per year

Quality: 🍷🍷🍷🍷🍷   Price: ★★★★ – ★★★★★

Best vintages: '71, '75, '76, '79, '82, '83, '85, '86, '88, '89, '90

Almost every top wine estate in the world, whether it be Château Lafite or Domaine de la Romanée Conti, has been through periods when its wines have failed to live up to their reputations. Weingut Joh. Jos. Prüm is a rare exception, having produced superb Riesling wines since the estate's foundation in 1911 right up to the present day. Since 1920 the estate has been run by just two members of the Prüm family: Sebastian Prüm, who built up the estate's name and developed the 'J. J.' style of wine-making, and since his sudden death in 1969 by the present owner, Dr Manfred Prüm.

At a first meeting Dr Manfred Prüm can give the impression of being a man who is not easily approachable. Unlike most Mosel wine producers he prefers not to show his cellar to visitors, and would always rather present mature wines than the latest vintage. However, with longer acquaintance he becomes the most charming and witty of hosts.

It is the wines from the great Wehlener Sonnenuhr site directly across the river Mosel from the estate house which have made Joh. Jos. Prüm's reputation. They have an exceptionally intense fruitiness, which often has slightly exotic overtones, are very racy, and have a bouquet as full and subtle as a garden of summer flowers. However, the wines from the estate's vineyards in the Zeltinger Sonnenuhr, which have a slight earthiness, the Graacher Himmelreich, which are a little broader and firmer, and the Bernkasteler Lay/Badstube, which are leaner and more piquant, are also of the highest quality. In the wines' extreme youth these differences tend to be somewhat obscured by a yeasty aroma which the wines retain for some time after bottling.

'It is very important that people shouldn't drink our wines as soon as they come on the market,' Dr Manfred advises, 'but should wait at least until the wines have been in the bottle for one year before starting to drink them.' This applies most of all to the finest late-harvested wines: the Auslese with gold capsules (the long gold capsule indicates the finest and richest Auslese wines), Beerenauslese, Trockenbeerenauslese, and Eiswein, which need much more time before they begin to show their full potential. Tasted very young these wines have a pronounced sweetness, which can be rather dominant. This, along with the 'spritz' of carbon dioxide to be found in all the Joh. Jos. Prüm wines, enables them to mature very slowly in the bottle. Tasted after between ten and twenty years of ageing the result is a wine of luscious fruitiness, sublime richness, and an aftertaste which just goes on and on and on.

SCHLOSS SAARSTEIN

Saar

Weingut Schloss Saarstein, 5512 Serrig

Estate bottled   25 acres of Riesling

80,000 bottles of Riesling per year

Quality: 🍇🍇🍇🍇   Price: ★★★ – ★★★★

Best vintages: '71, '76, '79, '82, '83, '85, '88, '89, '90

Schloss Saarstein is a most unusual Saar estate, since in contrast to the other top Riesling producers on the Saar their best wines are as often dry (Trocken and Halbtrocken) as in the traditional style. Normally Saar wines are just too lean to be attractive in a dry style, but the Schloss Saarstein dry Rieslings have an exceptional amount of substance. This buffers the typical steeliness of Saar Rieslings, making for harmonious dry wines.

Owners Dieter Ebert and his son Christian work the entire estate by themselves except for the harvest. They are able to do this because the majority of their vineyards immediately surround Schloss Saarstein, which stands on a hilltop with a dramatic view over the Saar valley. Each year they carry huge quantities of humus into the vineyards to improve the stony soil. This results in wines with a remarkable depth of extract. It also gives them an extremely pronounced fruity bouquet, which is sometimes of exotic fruits and sometimes of cassis.

WILLI SCHAEFER

Middle Mosel

Weingut Willi Schaefer, Hauptstrasse 130, 5550 Graach

Estate bottled   4 acres of Riesling

16,000 bottles of Riesling per year

Quality: 🍇🍇🍇🍇   Price: ★★ – ★★★

Best vintages: '71, '75, '76, '79, '81, '83, '85, '88, '89, '90

In contrast to Wehlen, where there is an entire row of famous estates within just one street, no large or famous estates are situated in the village of Graach. For this reason its wines have long lagged behind those of Wehlen and Bernkastel in prestige and reputation. Of the many small estates in Graach, that of Willi Schaefer stands out for the consistently high quality of the wines year in year out, though such is the modesty of Willi Schaefer Jr that he would be lost for words if you said so. He would just say that he has good vineyards and works conscientiously in the cellar.

Willi Schaefer's Rieslings are among the purest expressions of the firm, earthy–minerally Graach character, and even in lesser vintages the wines are packed with ripe fruit. Those from the Graacher Himmelreich site are more open and appealing in their youth than the bigger, more highly structured wines from the Graacher Domprobst. However, after they have been cellared for at least three or four years there is usually no contest, as the Domprobst wines slowly open up to reveal their full, profound depth.

C. VON SCHUBERT

See Maximin Grünhaus/C. von Schubert

SELBACH-OSTER

Middle Mosel

Weingut Selbach-Oster, Uferallee 23, 5553 Zeltingen

Estate bottled   12.5 acres of Riesling

60,000 bottles of Riesling per year

Quality: 🍇🍇🍇🍇   Price: ★★ – ★★★★

Best vintages: '71, '75, '76, '79, '82, '85, '88, '89, '90

Hans Selbach and his son Johannes run what is easily the top wine estate in the town of Zeltingen. Hans Selbach is one of the *grands seigneurs* of the Mosel region, with an enormous wealth of knowledge of the region's wines which he is only too glad to share, every judgement being carefully measured and considered. His dynamic son Johannes has recently returned from several years working for the German Wine Information Bureau in the USA.

The finest Rieslings from the Selbach-Oster estate are undoubtedly those from the Zeltinger Sonnenuhr site, which directly adjoins the Wehlener Sonnenuhr and is the last really top site on the continuous 'wall' of vines that cover the steep slopes between Bernkastel and Zeltingen. It gives wines which are slightly earthier but similar in structure to those of the Wehlener Sonnenuhr – extremely elegant and polished, with a clean racy finish. The extra touch of earth compared with Wehlen makes for good dry-style wines too, which have enough body and fruit to balance the pronounced acidity. The estate also has fine vineyards in Bernkastel, Graach, Wehlen, and the other sites of Zeltingen from which many classic Mosel Riesling wines are made.

WWE DR H. THANISCH (VDP)

Middle Mosel

Weingut Wwe Dr H. Thanisch, Saarallee 31, 5550 Bernkastel–Kues

Estate bottled   15 acres of Riesling

60,000 bottles of Riesling per year

Quality: ♦♦♦♦   Price: ★★★ – ★★★★★

Best vintages: '71, '75, '76, '88, '89, '90

Thanisch is one of the legendary names of the Middle Mosel, and after some years in the doldrums the estate is now making excellent wines once again. It is, however, essential to point out that as a result of the estate's division there are now *two* Thanisch estates. The one described here is that which is based in the Thanisch mansion house in Kues, and which is a member of the VDP quality wine estates association. Since the other Thanisch estate, owned by the Müller-Burggraef family, also uses the estate's traditional label it is important to look out for the VDP eagle emblem to identify the wines of the better estate of the two.

The estate is run by Sofia Knabben-Spier, a direct descendant of Dr Hugo Thanisch, after whom it is named. She is assisted by her husband Ulrich Spier, who teaches at the Bernkastel wine school, and by manager Norbert Breit. Since the 1987 vintage Herr Breit has been responsible for the cellar work, and from that year onwards there has been a dramatic improvement in the quality of the wines. 1988 was the first top vintage after the estate's new cellar in Kues was established, and their spectacular wines from the Bernkasteler Lay and the world-famous Bernkasteler Doctor site proved that the estate is now firmly on the right track to regain its reputation as one of Germany's leading Riesling wine producers. If the present momentum can be maintained, in a short time the Thanisch estate will certainly deserve a five-star rating.

DR WAGNER

Saar

Bahnhofstrasse 3, 5510 Saarburg

Estate bottled   18 acres of Riesling

80,000 bottles of Riesling per year

Quality: 🍷🍷🍷🍷   Price: ★★ – ★★★

Best vintages: '71, '75, '76, '79, '83, '84, '86, '87, '88, '90

Heinz Wagner's wines are full and earthy. They make a bold statement even in vintages which are extremely difficult for the Saar, such as 1984 and 1987. In fact it is then that Heinz Wagner makes his most beautifully balanced wines, full of ripe fruit and elegantly racy.

The consistency of the Wagner wines seems a direct expression of Heinz Wagner's character. A somewhat shy yet excitable middle-aged man, he would always rather be out in the vineyards or down in the cellar with his wines. He doesn't rush his wines into the bottle from the wooden casks where they are made, and often they don't come onto the market until a year after the harvest. In this and many other aspects of his wine-making, he sticks firmly to the traditional methods which he learnt in his youth.

WEGELER-DEINHARD

Middle Mosel and Ruwer

Gutsverwaltung Wegeler-Deinhard, Marterthal, 5550 Bernkastel–Kues

Estate bottled   75 acres of Riesling

300,000 bottles of Riesling per year

BERNKASTELER DOCTOR RIESLINGS

Quality: 🍇🍇🍇🍇   Price: ★★★★★

OTHER RIESLINGS

Quality: 🍇🍇🍇   Price: ★★★ – ★★★★

Best vintages: '71, '75, '76, '83, '86, '88, '90

Though the wines from Deinhard's estate on the Mosel are somewhat erratic in quality, impressive wines are produced regularly enough to make them an important producer on the Middle Mosel. The estate in Bernkastel is run by Norbert Kreuzberger, who has decades of experience in the region. However, the wines are not made on the Mosel but in Deinhard's central cellars in Koblenz. The jewels in Deinhard's Middle Mosel crown are undoubtedly their extensive vineyard holdings in the Wehlener Sonnenuhr, of which they are the largest owners with just over twelve acres, and the Bernkasteler Doctor. Their wines from both these great vineyards are of consistently high quality.

DR WEINS-PRÜM

Middle Mosel and Ruwer

Weingut Dr F. Weins-Prüm (Selbach-Weins), Uferallee 20, 5550 Bernkastel–Wehlen

Estate bottled   10.5 acres of Riesling

45,000 bottles of Riesling per year

Quality: 🍇🍇🍇🍇   Price: ★★ – ★★★★

Best vintages: '71, '75, '76, '79, '83, '85, '88, '89, '90

Often reticent and unforthcoming, Bert Selbach none the less makes wines which have great elegance and character. He has produced some of the most impressive Middle Mosel Rieslings during recent years, each vintage seeming to be slightly better made than the last. In the village of Wehlen, which is blessed with a large handful of good estates bearing the Prüm name, there is intense competition to be the best Riesling producer alongside Joh. Jos. Prüm. With his excellent 1988 vintage wines Bert Selbach has undoubtedly reached that position.

The Weins-Prüm wines are perfect examples of the classic Mosel Riesling balancing act, in which intense fruit flavours and some sweetness are set against mouth-watering acidity and complex mineral tones. The estate's vineyards are widely scattered, from a tiny plot in the Erdener Prälat, through the Ürziger Würzgarten, Wehlener Sonnenuhr and Klosterberg, and Graacher Himmelreich, to a sizeable parcel in the Waldracher Sonnenberg far away in the Ruwer valley.

ZILLIKEN

Saar

Weingut Forstmeister Geltz Zilliken, Heckingstrasse 20, 5510 Saarburg

Estate bottled   19 acres of Riesling

80,000 bottles of Riesling per year

RIESLING AUSLESE AND EISWEIN

Quality: 🍇🍇🍇🍇🍇   Price: ★★★★★

OTHER RIESLINGS

Quality: 🍇🍇🍇   Price: ★★★

Best vintages: '71, '75, '76, '79, '82, '83, '85, '88, '89, '90

Saar Rieslings always have a pronounced acidity which gives them a piquant tartness that is too severe for the taste of many wine-lovers but is avidly sought by numerous fanatics. Hanno Zilliken's Rieslings are definitely not for the casual wine drinker, since they are among the most extreme expressions of the steely Saar Riesling character. Here it is often necessary to harvest selectively in order to reach high quality levels, when on the warmer Middle Mosel such wines can be harvested direct from the vine. Along with Egon Müller, Hanno Zilliken is the most determined selective harvester in the region, and virtually every vintage he produces some remarkable dessert wines. In particular, he has produced a string of great ice wines and ice-wine-style Spätlese and Auslese wines from the top Saarburger Rausch site since 1980. These are incredible wines, with a fire and brilliance that can make them painful to sip in their extreme youth, but which gives them the potential to develop in the bottle for decades. Lovely, conventional-style Spätlese and Auslese wines from the Rausch and the Ockfener Bockstein sites with a slightly less extreme balance are also produced. Simple-quality wines from the estate can be rather hard and lean though.

Nahe

Total vineyard area: 11,300 acres

Vineyard area planted with Riesling: 23%/2,600 acres

Average annual Riesling production: 12,000,000 bottles

The Nahe tends to be regarded as an in-between region. Located between the much larger Mosel–Saar–Ruwer to the north and the Rhine regions to the east, and relatively small in size, it has had a hard job creating an identity for itself. The fact that there are several world-class Riesling producers here doesn't seem to have helped very much, for it is they who have become famous rather than the Nahe. The lack of a clearly dominant classic grape variety here, and the relatively great stylistic differences between the Riesling wines from different parts of the region, have certainly not helped it to build up its image.

The greatest Riesling wines from the Nahe are undoubtedly those of the winding Upper Nahe valley, which stretches from the massive porphyry Rotenfels cliffs at Traisen to Schloss-böckelheim and Monzingen. This is an extremely rocky region, with massive porphyry and melaphry rocks projecting from the steep hillsides. The vineyard soils are often extremely stony, and the Riesling wines reflect this in their racy, minerally character. The best wines from the top sites of the Upper Nahe have as much elegance and finesse as the greatest Mosel Ries-lings, combined with a bit more weight. They are extremely long-lived, and can still seem very youthful after five or more years in the bottle.

The Riesling wines from the more gently sloping vineyards round the large town of Bad Kreuznach, and its important viticultural suburb Wintzenheim, are full-bodied with a juicy fruitiness. Those from the villages between Bad Kreuznach and the Nahe's confluence with the Rhine at Bingen, and from the villages to the north-west of Bad Kreuznach such as Wallhausen, give wines that are quite Rheingau-like – medium-bodied, firm, and slightly earthy.

PAUL ANHEUSER

Middle and Upper Nahe

Weingut Paul Anheuser, Stromberger Strasse 15–19, 6550 Bad Kreuznach

Estate bottled   95 acres of Riesling

300,000 bottles of Riesling per year

Quality: 🍇🍇🍇   Price: ★★ – ★★★★

Best vintages: '71, '75, '76, '79, '85, '89, '90

The Paul Anheuser estate is presently the most consistent of the three large privately owned estates on the Nahe. Their Rieslings come from vineyards widely scattered along the river and in its side valleys. Peter Anheuser makes good solid traditional-style and dry-style Riesling wines which are fermented and matured in wooden casks in his extensive cellars in Bad Kreuznach. Before Peter Anheuser took up the reins in 1969 the estate produced only dry wines, which had earned it the nickname 'Sour Paul'. In fact the dry wines produced by the estate are not at all sour, but are full-bodied for German dry wines, with plenty of earthy fruitiness and harmonious acidity. The traditional-style wines have modest sweetness and full succulent fruit. The estate's most elegant wines are those of Niederhausen and Schlossböckelheim on the Upper Nahe. The best of the Bad Kreuznach wines are generally those from the Krötenpfuhl site.

CRUSIUS

Upper Nahe

Weingut Hans Crusius & Sohn, Hauptstrasse 2, 6551 Traisen

Estate bottled   24.5 acres of Riesling

64,000 bottles of Riesling per year

Quality: 🍇🍇🍇🍇🍇   Price: ★★★ – ★★★★

Best vintages: '71, '75, '76, '79, '83, '85, '86, '88, '89, '90

The Crusius estate has gone from strength to strength in recent years, and there can be no doubt that Hans and Dr Peter Crusius are at present among the top Riesling wine producers on the Nahe. In each of the last vintages they have turned out impeccable collections of dry, medium-dry, and traditional-style Rieslings, with the 1989 vintage perhaps their best since the stellar 1976s. Indeed, few Riesling producers in the Rhine regions can match the consistent excellence of their wines.

Little wonder that by each mid-summer 'Sold Out' is stamped all over the list offering the new vintage.

Perhaps their most remarkable Riesling wines, with an astonishingly complex spicy-minerally intensity, are those from the Traiser Bastei site. This extremely small site, a mere two and a half acres of vines, is sandwiched between the towering mass of the Rotenfels cliffs and the river Nahe. Such is the micro-climate here that wines of at least Spätlese quality are harvested almost every vintage. They are currently fermented dry. The Riesling wines of the Schlossböckelheimer Felsenberg site from further up-river are richly fruity, spicy and elegant. They are vinified in the traditional style, and are likewise invariably of Spätlese quality. Somewhat leaner and racier, with a vibrant, piquant fruitiness, are the Traiser Rotenfels Riesling wines, which are made in both the dry and traditional styles.

HERMANN DÖNNHOF

Upper Nahe

Weingut Hermann Dönnhof, Bahnhofstrasse 11, 6551 Oberhausen

Estate bottled   16 acres of Riesling

50,000 bottles of Riesling per year

Quality: 🍇🍇🍇🍇🍇   Price: ★★ – ★★★★

Best vintages: '71, '76, '79, '83, '86, '88, '89, '90

Directly across the Nahe from the State Domaine (p. 117) are the small village of Oberhausen and the Hermann Dönnhof estate. In recent years the competition between the two to produce the finest collection of wines from each vintage has been intense. With the State Domaine currently experiencing problems, there can be no doubt that Helmut Dönnhof is making the greatest Nahe wines.

Helmut Dönnhof mixes a traditional style of wine-making in wooden casks with some modern technology. Each cask is bottled separately, and since he owns vineyards in seven different sites and ferments some of each dry, medium-dry, and with residual sweetness, this makes for a huge range of wines. While the dry wines are very well made, they are too severe for most non-German palates. The elegantly dry-tasting Halb-trocken (medium-dry) wines show extremely well-defined fruit flavours and very clear vineyard character. The wines with residual sweetness, and particularly those from the Nieder-hauser Hermannshöhle, and Dönnhof's monopole Oberhäuser Brücke, have a truly sublime interplay of subtly sweet intense fruitiness and racy acidity. They are archetypal Nahe wines.

SCHLOSSGUT DIEL

Lower Nahe

Schlossgut Diel, 6531 auf Burg Layen

Estate bottled   18 acres of Riesling

60,000 bottles of Riesling per year

Quality: 🍾🍾🍾🍾   Price: ★★★ – ★★★★

Best vintages: '71, '75, '76, '79, '83, '86, '89, '90

Visiting Schlossgut Diel for the first time is a mind-boggling and eye-boggling experience. As you arrive you notice that in front of the ultra-traditional estate house stand a number of brightly coloured modern sculptures that look like strange plants waiting for something dramatic to happen. Inside the house post-modern furniture stands cheek by jowl with beautiful Art Deco originals, and the kitschy nineteenth-century wrought-iron banisters to the main staircase have been 'electrified' with dazzling primary colours. However, none of this is enough to prepare the visitor for the shock he receives in the cellar. Every square inch of the walls, ceilings, and floors, and the steel fermentation tanks have all been painted with strange yet compelling designs.

Since 1987 Armin Diel has transformed both the Schlossgut

Diel wines and the estate. The innumerable modern vine crossings which once filled the estate's vineyards are all gone. For a
number of years Diel produced only dry wines, and matured
one of his Rieslings in new oak. Only very recently has he
returned to making some traditional-style Riesling wines.

For many in the German wine scene this is all a case of too
much French influence, and they point to the numerous visits
to the French wine regions which Armin Diel has made as a
writer for the important German wine magazine *Alles Über
Wein*. Armin Diel openly accepts that he has learnt from the
French: 'When I look at the huge range of wines produced by
most of the best German wine estates and I compare this with a
Bordeaux *château* which makes one or two wines each year I
know which is easier for wine drinkers to understand, and for
the producer to sell.' Consequently only the Rieslings from
Diel's top vineyard sites, Dorsheimer Pittermännchen and
Dorsheimer Goldloch, are sold with these vineyard designations, the Pittermännchen wines having a floral Mosel-like
quality, and the Goldloch firmer and deeper in flavour. The
estate's other wines are sold under the estate name.

STATE DOMAINE
NIEDERHAUSEN-SCHLOSSBÖCKELHEIM

Upper, Middle, and Lower Nahe

Verwaltung der Staatlichen Weinbaudomänen
Niederhausen-Schlossböckelheim, 6551 Oberhausen

Estate bottled   99 acres of Riesling

300,000 bottles of Riesling per year

Quality: 🍇🍇🍇🍇   Price: ★★★ – ★★★★★

Best vintages: '71, '75, '76, '79, '83, '85, '88

The Nahe State Domaine remains the finest state wine
domaine in Germany. There is no doubt though that since the
departure of its erstwhile wine-maker Karl-Heinz Sattelmayer

it is not quite what it once was. During the 'Sattelmayer period' the consistency with which the domaine turned out excellent wines year after year was truly astonishing. Sadly, after the 1989 harvest, Herr Sattelmayer's successor, who was just beginning to get a really firm grip on the wine-making, left, and the future quality of the domaine's wines hangs in the balance.

The State Domaine's wines have always been very racy, with finely nuanced fruit, plenty of extract, and an intense minerally character. The domaine is famous for traditional-style Riesling wines with some sweetness, but their balance has always been so impeccable that to call them sweet would be an insult. The greatest wines from the domaine are those from the Schloss-böckelheimer Kupfergrube and the barely less tongue-twisting Niederhauser Hermannsberg and Hermannshöhle sites. The State Domaine was founded in 1902 by the Prussian govern-ment, and many of its vineyards, including the steep terraced Kupfergrube, were created from arid rocky scrub land. The aridity remains a problem and effects a severe natural reduction in the yield, which has much to do with the wines' intensity.

Rheingau

Total vineyard area: 7,250 acres

Vineyard area planted with Riesling: 81%/5,900 acres

Average annual Riesling production: 25,000,000 bottles

The Rheingau is perhaps the most famous of Germany's Ries-ling wine-producing regions, and of all these regions it is the most successful at marketing itself. Its high reputation and marketing success are due to several important factors. It is a relatively small region incapable of significant expansion, where the two traditional grape varieties – Riesling for white wines and Spätburgunder (Pinot Noir) for red wines – almost completely dominate the vineyard plantations. It is also home to a dozen estates with eighty or more acres of vineyards in aristocratic ownership. Lastly, it has a captive local market in the cities of Wiesbaden, Frankfurt, Mainz and the surrounding industrial towns.

There is no denying that very professional marketing has recently been added to this list of pluses, and that as a result the Rheingau sells its Riesling wines more easily than any other region of Germany. Sadly this success has led to an all too relaxed attitude towards quality on the part of many estate owners and directors in the region. While there are large numbers of good Riesling wine producers in the region, it is extremely difficult to find traditional-style Riesling wines (with residual sweetness) to match the best wines in that style from the Mosel–Saar–Ruwer, or dry Riesling wines which can match the best wines in that style from the Rheinpfalz or the Rhine Front area of Rheinhessen.

Despite these criticisms, there are some encouraging developments in the Rheingau. Most obvious among these is the Charta Estates Association, which was founded in 1984 by Dr Hans Ambrosi, director of the region's State Wine Domaine, the late Prof. Dr Helmut Becker of the wine school and research station in Geisenheim, Bernhard Breuer of the Georg Breuer estate and Scholl & Hillebrand shipping house in Rüdesheim, and Graf Matuschka-Greiffenclau of the Schloss Vollrads and Fürst Löwenstein estates. The Charta has concentrated all its energies on promoting drier-style Rheingau Riesling wines from member estates which have passed a strict set of quality and style control tests. While harmoniously dry for most non-German palates, the Charta Riesling wines need several years in bottle to become really appealing. As the makers intend, they are 'gastronomic wines' which invariably show their best with food.

Although the Charta association's assertion that dry wines are *the* traditional style of the region has much truth in it, I think that things were always a little more complex than this statement would lead one to believe. In lesser and average vintages the great majority of the region's wines certainly fermented through to dryness. However, those producers with deep cold cellars, where the fermentation was slower and less energetic, must have had many barrels of wine with a slight sweetness almost every year. This continues to happen today. In the top vintages I'm sure that the majority of the region's Riesling wines were not bone-dry, and retained a noticeable sweetness. So while heartily concurring with the Charta members' dismissal of the often over-sweetened wines of the sixties and seventies, I think that a place remains for Rheingau Riesling wines with some residual sweetness, particularly from Spätlese quality upwards.

It was the Rheingau which pioneered the production of late-harvested Riesling wines from grapes affected by noble rot. They created the designations 'Spätlese' (late harvest), 'Auslese' (select late harvest), 'Beerenauslese' (selected berry late harvest), and 'Trockenbeerenauslese' (shrivelled berry late harvest). This tradition of strict selective harvesting to produce small quantities of fine dessert wines has, with the exception of a handful of estates, been lost. If Rheingau Rieslings of the regular quality grades (QbA and Kabinett) have a firm rather earthy character that some find too austere, the rare dessert wines made from Riesling in the Rheingau have a scintillating interplay of acidity and concentrated, honeyed fruit that only the wines on the Nahe and Mosel–Saar–Ruwer can match.

J. B. BECKER

Weingut J. B. Becker, Rheinstrasse 6, 6620 Walluf

Estate bottled   21.5 acres of Riesling

78,000 bottles of Riesling per year

Quality: 🍷🍷🍷🍷🍷   Price: ★★★ – ★★★★

Best vintages: '71, '75, '76, '79, '83, '88, '89, '90

Hans-Josef Becker is an extreme individualist and doesn't suffer fools gladly. However, behind his somewhat intimidating manner and magnificent moustache is a committed, highly traditional wine-maker. His Rieslings, which are mostly produced in the drier styles (Trocken and Halbtrocken), have more character than those of any other estate at the eastern end of the Rheingau. For dry wines with only 10° to 11° of alcohol they have a remarkable depth and length of flavour. These are dry white wines which are light only in alcohol, *not* in fruit or extract.

The first dry Riesling wines were produced at the Becker estate fully twenty years ago, principally because they are the personal preference of Hans-Josef and of his sister Maria, who administers the estate. The yield from the Riesling vines in the Beckers' best vineyards – in the Wallufer Walkenberg, Eltviller Sonnenberg, and Rauenthaler Wulfen – is very modest, and this combined with long maturation in large wooden casks in the estates gives the wines an excellent harmony, in spite of their abundant acidity.

The Beckers are both almost fanatically hard workers, and it is quite remarkable how much of the work in the estate they do themselves, given its size. On top of this they run a wine-broking business, and The Wine Garden, an outdoor wine bar just across the road from their home almost directly on the bank of the Rhine – the perfect place to taste the superb dry Becker Rieslings.

HANS HERMANN ESER

Hans Hermann Eser, Weingut Johannishof, 6222
   Johannisberg

Estate bottled   45 acres of Riesling

165,000 bottles of Riesling per year

Quality: 🍇🍇🍇🍇   Price: ★★ – ★★★★

Best vintages: '71, '75, '76, '79, '83, '85, '86, '88, '89

Hans Hermann Eser is one of the most reliable producers of Riesling wines in the entire Rheingau. Perhaps because his estate is not too large and it is therefore possible for him to keep an extremely tight grip on everything in the vineyards and cellar, and perhaps because of the strength of commitment of every member of the Eser family, the estate regularly out-classes some of its famous neighbours in the region. The Esers have an extremely clear philosophy, stretching from the vineyards to the wine in the bottle, and all their wines are marked by the classic raciness which has made the name of Johannisberg synonymous with fine Riesling wine around the world. They all boast a brilliant interplay of piquant acidity and intense, finely nuanced fruit. The estate's Charta Riesling wines (harmoniously dry) have a brilliance and finesse which make them among the very best wines made in this style. They are perfectly suited to accompanying all kinds of fish dishes. The traditional-style wines have only a modest touch of sweetness and enormous ageing potential.

The Eser family are traditionalists in the very best sense. The many recent modernizations in the estate have been undertaken with great care to ensure that a continuity with the past is always maintained. Although Hans Hermann Eser has a modern cellar filled with stainless-steel tanks, the best wines all ferment in wooden casks in the extremely cold vaulted cellar cut deep into the hillside behind the estate house, and even the lesser wines which are fermented in tanks always spend some time maturing in barrel.

GRAF VON KANITZ

Weingut Graf von Kanitz, Rheinstrasse 49, 6223 Lorch

Estate bottled   40 acres of Riesling

100,000 bottles of Riesling per year

Quality: 🍇🍇🍇🍇   Price: ★★★ – ★★★★

Best vintages: '71, '75, '76, '79, '83, '85, '86, '89, '90

It is a credit to its director Gernot Boos that the Graf von Kanitz estate should now rank among the top estates of the

Rheingau. This is a remarkable achievement considering that Lorch is very much the forgotten corner of the Rheingau. It is situated at the very western extremity of the region, its vineyards lying on the right bank of the river just north of where it enters the narrow gorge whose castles and precipitous vineyards have made the Rhine famous. Here the soils are completely different from those in the main body of the Rheingau, being composed of slate and quartzite. This gives wines with a racy acidity that are always vibrantly fruity. Even in lesser vintages it is possible to produce very attractive light, dry Rieslings here. The von Kanitz estate is the specialist for this style, and there are few producers in the Rheingau who can match them.

There can be little doubt that the reason for the remarkably consistent quality of the Kanitz wines is the personal commitment of Gernot Boos. He runs the estate as if it was his own. As early as 1968 he began converting to organic viticulture, and since that date the vineyards haven't been ploughed once. Instead the weeds are allowed to grow through the winter and into the spring, then knocked down once the vines begin to grow. It is to be hoped that after Herr Boos's forthcoming retirement his successor will maintain the estate's high standards.

SCHLOSS JOHANNISBERG

Schloss Johannisberg, 6222 Johannisberg

Estate bottled   86 acres of Riesling

280,000 bottles of Riesling per year

Quality: ♦♦♦   Price: ★★★★ – ★★★★★

Best vintages: '71, '75, '76, '79, '85, '88, '89, '90

Schloss Johannisberg occupies a very special place in the history of Riesling wines. It was here that vineyards were first planted with 100 per cent Riesling, and here that the late-harvesting of Riesling grapes to make naturally sweet wines was discovered.

However, great wines don't come about as a result of past achievements – or by being owned by Prince von Metternich (and the German industrial concern Oetker) – but are rather the product of a carefully thought-out and strict policy in both the vineyard and the cellar. For several years at the beginning of the 1980s Schloss Johannisberg seemed to lose its hitherto magic touch, and the wines seemed to lack that miraculous combination of lightness, strength, and finesse which made those from the top vintages of previous decades so sensational.

Thankfully, under the management of Director Wolfgang Schleicher there have been steady improvements during the last few years, and the quality of most of the wines produced today is again high.

The Schloss Johannisberg vineyards immediately surround the baroque Schloss, which was built by the Prince Bishop of Fulda shortly after his purchase of the estate in 1716. The Schloss was rebuilt in 1757–9, but the original cellars remain. The new, recently completed, cellar with its serried ranks of stainless-steel tanks is not meant as a substitute for the beautiful cask cellar under the castle, but rather as a complement to it. It certainly increases Schloss Johannisberg's potential to make great wines. Visiting the Schloss it is hard not to be bowled over by the grandeur of the buildings, the magnificent view from the terrace in front of the Schloss, and the centuries of tradition stretching back to the first mention of viticulture here in 817.

FREIHERR ZU KNYPHAUSEN

Weingut Freiherr zu Knyphausen, Klosterhof Drais, 6228 Erbach

Estate bottled   32 acres of Riesling

112,000 bottles of Riesling per year

Quality: 🍇🍇🍇   Price: ★★★–★★★★

Best vintages: '71, '75, '76, '79, '83, '85, '88, '89

Gerko Freiherr zu Knyphausen must be the only wine-grower and the only aristocrat in Germany to have a totem pole set in front of his house. The primitive style of this carving fits in curiously well with the medieval architecture of Klosterhof Drais, which was built in 1141 and is the Knyphausen family residence.

Gerko Freiherr zu Knyphausen and his Riesling wines are reserved yet sophisticated. They are classical Rheingau Rieslings, always a little austere in their youth, but with a vivid fruit and good ageing potential. If anything prevents this estate from reaching the very highest quality level, it is the relatively small acreages which it possesses in the top sites Erbacher Marcobrunn, Erbacher Siegelsberg, and Hattenheimer Wisselbrunnen. These are usually the estate's best wines, but also the first to sell out.

Gerko Knyphausen is a great fan of harmoniously dry Rheingau Rieslings in the Halbtrocken and Charta styles. 'For me most of the bone-dry Riesling wines of this region are too one-sided,' he told me, 'the acidity is a little too dominant. In contrast, the wines which haven't quite fermented to bone-dryness are much fruitier without tasting sweet. These are wonderful wines to drink either with a meal or on their own. I think that this is really the classic style of my region.'

FRANZ KÜNSTLER

Weingut Franz Künstler, Freiherr-vom-Stein-Ring 3, 6203 Hochheim

Estate bottled   12.5 acres of Riesling

50,000 bottles of Riesling per year

Quality: 🍇🍇🍇🍇🍇   Price: ★★★ – ★★★★

Best vintages: '75, '76, '79, '83, '85, '88, '89, '90

While the Rheingau Staatsweingüter and several of the famous aristocratic wine estates in the region stagger from one mediocre vintage to the next, a handful of family-owned estates are producing Rheingau Rieslings of stunning quality. The least known of these, and the most exciting, is the Franz Künstler estate in Hochheim.

Franz Künstler came to Germany from the wine village of Südmahrens in Czechoslovakia as a refugee in 1945. After studying at the Weinsberg wine school in Württemberg and working as the wine-maker in Hochheim for fifteen years, he established his own estate in 1965. The wines he made during the sixties and seventies were already of an impressive standard, but since his son Gunter has worked with him in the vineyards and cellar the estate has been producing world-class wines. The majority of the Künstler Rieslings are vinified dry (they are leading members of the Charta association) or medium-dry. All have a remarkable richness for dry German wines, with full citrus and peach fruit overlaid by complex earthy tones. The top dry wines – the Auslese Trocken and Spätlese Charta – are packed with extract and have enough structure to age for decades.

Only twenty-eight years of age and brimming with both energy and ideas, Gunter Künstler has already achieved an astonishing amount. I await the wines he will make during the nineties with bated breath.

LANGWERTH VON SIMMERN

Freiherrlich Langwerth von Simmern'sches Rentamt, Lang- werther Hof, Kirchgasse, 6228 Eltville

Estate bottled   90 acres of Riesling

300,000 bottles of Riesling per year

Quality: 🍇🍇🍇🍇   Price: ★★★ – ★★★★★

Best vintages: '71, '73, '75, '76, '79, '82, '83, '89, '90

Langwerth von Simmern is undoubtedly one of the great estates of the Rheingau, and has been for at least forty years. Until recently it has produced beautifully fruity Riesling wines year in year out. Von Simmern's forte has always been the traditional style of Rheingau Riesling with a touch of sweetness. While many estates overdid the sweetness during the sixties and seventies, Langwerth von Simmern held a very steady line, balancing the wines with as little sweetness as possible. As a result of this, and extremely careful work in the cellar by Josef Schell, they have always had a very finely nuanced fruitiness and perfect balance. Sadly, during the eighties quality at the estate has wavered. It is to be hoped that the most recent vintages represent a return to form.

Although the estate's most sought-after wines have always been its Rieslings from the famous Erbacher Marcobrunn, Rauenthaler Baiken (of which they are the best producer), and Hattenheimer Nussbrunnen, the site which was the origin of the estate regularly produces some of their finest wines. This is the Hattenheimer Mannberg, which was given to Johann Langwerth von Simmern in 1464 by Ludwig Herzog von Pfalz-Zweibrücken.

DR HEINRICH NÄGLER

Weingut Dr Heinrich Nägler, Friedrichstrasse 22, 6220 Rüdesheim

Estate bottled   14.5 acres of Riesling

45,000 bottles of Riesling per yea.

Quality: 🍇🍇🍇🍇   Price: ★★★ – ★★★★

Best vintages: '71, '75, '76, '79, '83, '85, '88, '89

Dr Heinrich Nägler produces fine-quality Riesling wines from the steeply sloping vineyards of the Rüdesheimer Berg in the traditional style with residual sweetness, as well as in the dry and medium-dry styles (Trocken and Halbtrocken). The 'sweet' wines are wonderful examples of how well-made Rheingau Riesling wines with residual sweetness don't taste sweet at all. They have good concentration and great elegance, and the finest need five or more years in the bottle to give their best. The near perfect exposition of the precipitously steep

Rüdesheimer Berg sites – Berg Rottland, Berg Roseneck, and Berg Schlossberg – facing south to south-west, makes for extremely ripe grapes from which the Näglers also make some beautiful dry wines. Their 1985 Rüdesheimer Berg Schlossberg Riesling Spätlese Trocken won second prize, against tough competition from Alsace and the New World, in the 1988 Olympiade du Vin, organized by the French gourmet magazine *Gault Millau*. A well-deserved accolade for a classic Nägler dry Riesling, a wine bursting with ripe fruit.

SCHLOSS REINHARTSHAUSEN

Schloss Reinhartshausen, 6229 Erbach

Estate bottled   132.5 acres of Riesling

465,000 bottles of Riesling per year

Quality: 🍇🍇🍇🍇

Price: ★★★ – ★★★★

Best vintages: '71, '75, '76, '79, '89, '90

Since 1988 the famous Schloss Reinhartshausen estate of the Princes of Prussia has been largely owned by Willy Leibbrand, owner of the eponymous German supermarket group. This takeover may turn out to be a very good thing, as the estate had been under-performing for some time. Instead of concentrating on producing the best possible Riesling wines, it seemed for many years that its managers were spending too much time on other grape varieties – Spätburgunder (Pinot Noir), Weiss-burgunder (Pinot Blanc), Chardonnay, Traminer, and Kerner – and on superficial new marketing ideas. Whatever the real problems were, the wines from the vintages of the early eighties didn't match estate director Dr Zerbe's sincere commitment to quality.

Thankfully there have been dramatic improvements during the last few years, and the estate's wines are now consistently impressive. The wine-making remains traditional in that the wines are all matured in wood – and often for much longer than the six months typical of the region today. In common with those of the other large estates in the region, Schloss Reinhartshausen's Riesling wines are vinified dry and medium-dry as well as in the traditional sweeter style.

The estate is one of the major owners of the famous Erbacher Marcobrunn site, as well as exclusively owning the adjoining Erbacher Schlossberg and good-sized portions of the neighbouring Erbacher Siegelsberg, Hattenheimer Wisselbrunnen and Nussbrunnen sites. Not surprisingly it is the wines from these sites which are the most interesting.

SCHLOSS SCHÖNBORN

Domänenweingut Schloss Schönborn, 6228 Hattenheim

Estate bottled   116 acres of Riesling

360,000 bottles of Riesling per year

Quality: ꙮꙮꙮꙮ   Price: ★★★ – ★★★★★

Best vintages: '71, '76, '83, '86, '88, '89, '90

For many years the estate of Dr Karl Graf von Schönborn regularly failed to achieve the high quality which its superb vineyard holdings in many of the Rheingau's top sites should have made possible. The wines were often too sweet and seemed to lack a bit of real depth. If the wines of the last few years have still been a little erratic, there can be no doubt that the standard has leapt up to another league since the middle of the eighties. At present no other estate in the Rheingau produces traditional-style Spätlese and Auslese wines which match the best from the Schönborn estate. They have a concentration, power, and richness against which the wines from the other noble estates seem weak. Sadly, their drier-style wines have been very mixed in quality, some being unbalanced.

The reason for this dramatic turnaround in the estate's fortunes is the new policy which director Robert Englert introduced five years ago. The lesser vineyards and those not planted with either Riesling or Spätburgunder (Pinot Noir) were sold or leased away. The estate shrank by over forty acres, so that only good to great vineyard sites remain. The yield has also been substantially reduced, the best sites having been pruned to give as little as half the yield normally taken from Riesling vineyards in the region.

Although the estate makes great wines from the Rüdesheimer Berg vineyards, from Hochheim at the eastern extremity of the Rheingau, and from various sites in the middle of the region, its best wines generally come from the top sites close to its base in Hattenheim. From old vines in the famous Erbacher Marcobrunn site they produce what are perhaps the most complex and minerally of all Rheingau Rieslings. Similar in quality, but totally different in style, are the extrovert wines from their monopole Hattenheimer Pfaffenberg site, which have a huge peachy bouquet overlaid with exotic fruit tones and a seductive lush fruit on the palate.

SCHLOSS VOLLRADS & FÜRST LÖWENSTEIN

Schloss Vollrads, 6227 Oestrich-Winkel

Schloss Vollrads

Estate bottled   120 acres of Riesling
400,000 bottles of Riesling per year

Fürst Löwenstein

Estate bottled   47.5 acres of Riesling
150,000 bottles of Riesling
Quality: 🍇🍇🍇   Price: ★★★ – ★★★★
Best vintages (from both estates): '71, '75, '76, '79, '83, '85, '89, '90

Schloss Vollrads is the oldest family-owned wine business in the world and possibly the oldest family-owned business of any kind. The family of owner Erwein Graf Matuschka-Greiffen-clau have been selling wine from their vineyards above the town of Winkel since at least 1211. All family businesses go through their ups and downs, and when Erwein took over the family estate after the death of his father Graf Richard in 1975 there was a great deal of work to be done to rebuild it. The fabric of the Schloss was crumbling, fully one third of the vineyards had been planted with inferior new grape varieties, and the cellars were in a chaotic state. Since then Erwein Graf Matuschka has restored the entire complex of buildings, brought the vineyard plantations back up to 98 per cent Riesling, and completely renovated the cellars.

Having been Olivetti's marketing director in Germany before returning to the Schloss, Graf Matuschka has brought with him modern marketing of the highest sophistication. His principal strategy in rebuilding the estate's name has been to stage innumerable dinners and presentations round the world to demonstrate that semi-dry (Halbtrocken) Rheingau Ries-lings are ideal wines to accompany fine cuisine.

For years, together with Egbert Engelhardt, the chef at his Michelin star-rated Graues Haus restaurant in Winkel, he has studied the marrying of food and wine. 'The most important thing in combining wine and food,' he told me, 'is to remember two very simple rules: the intensity of flavour of food and wine should match, and the sweetness and acidity in food and wine should balance.'

Although he also produces bone-dry (Trocken) and conven-tional-style wines with residual sweetness, it is the semi-dry direction which dominates the estate's production and which he considers an ideal accompaniment to modern cooking. Each vintage, the best wines in this style are sold as Charta Rieslings, and year in year out they are the estate's finest wines. All the Vollrads wines have a firm steely structure and need at least two years in the bottle for this to become a piquant racy fruitiness that cuts the richness of cream or reduced sauces perfectly.

Graf Matuschka has leased the Fürst Löwenstein estate in Hallgarten since 1979. Its Riesling wines are a little broader and quicker to develop than those of Schloss Vollrads. They are made at the Schloss and marketed in a similar manner to the Vollrads wines.

WEGELER-DEINHARD

Gutsverwaltung Wegeler-Deinhard, Friedensplatz 9–11, 6227 Oestrich-Winkel

Estate bottled   140 acres of Riesling

520,000 bottles of Riesling per year

GEHEIMRAT J AND RIESLING EISWEIN

Quality: 🍇🍇🍇🍇   Price: ★★★★★

OTHER RIESLINGS

Quality: 🍇🍇🍇   Price: ★★★

Best vintages: '71, '75, '76, '79, '83, '85, '86, '88, '89

Of Deinhard's three large wine estates in Germany that in the Rheingau is probably the best. Director Norbert Holderrieth runs this estate as if it were his own, and Deinhard have given him a very free hand to do as he considers right. In fact, with director of wine-making at Deinhard Manfred Völpel, he oversees the production at all three of the Deinhard estates. Together they have turned the estate over to producing almost exclusively dry wines (Trocken and Charta) during the last five years. Traditional-style wines with some residual sugar are also made for export, but the estate should really be judged on its best dry Riesling wines.

'We can't be all things to all people,' says Norbert Holderrieth. 'We have to concentrate our energies in a certain direction and seek to perfect those styles.' The most obvious expression of the direction in which the estate has concentrated its efforts is the luxury dry Riesling *cuvée* Geheimrat J, which the estate has produced since the 1983 vintage. This is a blend of the best casks of dry Riesling from each suitable vintage.

Criticized by some as too obvious a copy of de Ladoucette's luxury *cuvée* Pouilly-Fumé Baron de L, it has none the less been a runaway success and supply cannot begin to keep pace with demand. Next to the Geheimrat J the estate's Charta Riesling wines are of excellent quality, racy, with vivid fruit and plenty of substance for dry-style Rheingau Rieslings.

The traditional-style wines are very good examples of their type, elegant and barely sweeter than off-dry. The exceptions to this are the great ice wines which Wegeler-Deinhard produce in every suitable vintage. They are intensely sweet, but the sweetness is cut by enormous acidity, which gives these exciting dessert wines great ageing potential.

ROBERT WEIL

Weingut Robert Weil, Mühlberg 5, 6229 Kiedrich

Estate bottled   87 acres of Riesling

300,000 bottles of Riesling per year

Quality: 🍇🍇🍇🍇   Price: ★★★ – ★★★★

Best vintages: '71, '75, '76, '79, '83, '85, '88, '89

The purchase of the renowned Dr Weil estate from the Weil family in 1988 by the new joint venture of Graf Matuschka of Schloss Vollrads and the Japanese liquor giant Suntory Ltd was a major shock to the German wine industry. However, all the signs are that the new owners are making substantial invest-ments with the aim of rebuilding its reputation as one of the region's very top estates. The vineyards were substantially expanded in the first year to make Robert Weil the tenth largest vineyard owner in the region. The marketing of the wines has been re-thought too, almost all of them now being sold under the estate name. The half-timbered estate house, which was built by the Englishman Baron Sutton in the middle of the last century, is also about to be restored.

Director Wilhelm Weil, who is twenty-seven, is the estate's point of continuity with the past. He is responsible for both the vineyards and the wine-making at Robert Weil, as he was before the sale of the estate. He will continue to make the estate's Riesling wines much as in the past. At their best they were always among the most subtle and filigree of all Rheingau wines, with a pronounced racy acidity. Kiedrich lies high above the Rhine, its best vineyards covering a quite steep south-west-facing slope. The favourable micro-climate and stony soils here are responsible for the special character of the wines.

WERNER'SCHES DOMDECHANT

Domdechant Werner'sches Weingutes, Rathausstrasse 30, 6203 Hochheim

Estate bottled   28.5 acres of Riesling

100,000 bottles of Riesling per year

Quality: ♔♔♔♔   Price: ★★★ – ★★★★

Best vintages: '71, '76, '79, '83, '85, '88, '90

Hochheim is a paradox, since it is the origin of the generic term for Rhine wines, 'Hock', yet it is situated on the river Main at the eastern extremity of the Rheingau. The Riesling wines of Hochheim are also quite unlike those from the main body of the Rheingau, or any other of the Rhine regions. Full-bodied, mouth-filling, with an earthy fruitiness, they are wines which you either love or loathe.

The Rieslings from Dr Franz Werner Michel's estate are the most elegant Hochheimers but strongly marked with this special character from the heavy soils and warm micro-climate of Hochheim. Dr Michel is no great fan of dry German wines, yet to non-German palates his are among the most supple and harmonious dry wines in the Rheingau. The estate's traditional-style wines are, in common with all the better Hochheim Rieslings, *big* wines. 'Although we make all our wines in wooden casks in a very traditional manner,' Dr Michel told me, 'we still want them to be very clean and fruity, not clumsy or woody.'

Rheinhessen

Total vineyard area: 38,650 acres

Vineyard area planted with Riesling: 11%/4,225 acres

Average annual Riesling production: 20,000,000 bottles

Most of Rheinhessen is made up of rolling hills where viticulture has traditionally been only a part of mixed agriculture. The exceptions to this are the north-western corner of the region round Bingen and Ingelheim, and the eastern edge of the region between Nackenheim and Oppenheim (the Rhine Front) where there are steeply sloping vineyards which have long been extensively planted with Riesling. These are every bit as much classical wine-producing regions as the Rheingau, and their Riesling wines can be every bit as good as the best Rheingau wines.

The style of the region's Riesling wines is very varied owing to the huge differences in soil type and micro-climate. The majority of them, from the hinterland of the region, are rather hard and earthy – hearty wines that lack some elegance. Those from Bingen and Ingelheim are the most Rheingau-like, the Riesling wines of Oppenheim are quite rich and broad, and those from the top vineyard sites of Nierstein the most elegant and finely nuanced. Here it is essential to point out that the cheap generic wines from Rheinhessen sold under the names Binger St Rochuskapelle, Niersteiner Gutes Domtal, and Oppenheimer Krötenbrunnen are in no way comparable with the fine Riesling wines of the region. Invariably these generic wines are blends of wines from inferior wine varieties. Clean and reasonably fruity they may be, but they are never more than simple quaffing wines.

GUNDERLOCH

Weingut Gunderloch, Carl-Gunderloch-Platz 1, 6506 Nackenheim

Estate bottled   24 acres of Riesling

58,000 bottles of Riesling

Quality: 🍇🍇🍇🍇   Price: ★★★ – ★★★★

Best vintages: '87, '88, '89, '90

Fritz and Agnes Hasselbach of Nackenheim, immediately to the north of Nierstein, are the rising stars of Rheinhessen. Nackenheim isn't exactly the most famous wine village along the Rhine valley, but its Rothenberg site is one of the greatest vineyard sites along the entire length of the Rhine. It is the Hasselbachs' Rothenberg Rieslings which have virtually over-night made their reputation.

Half of the secret of this dramatic success is the radical reduction in yields which the estate introduced from the middle of the eighties. 'The most important thing for us was not just to get more sugar in the grapes,' explains Fritz, 'but to make more concentrated wines, wines which have more of everything.' The richness of fruit, substance, and long aftertaste that this policy gives their wines is complemented by a remarkable refinement, which is the product of careful and extremely patient cellar work. 'Some of our wines smell awful when they are very young,' Agnes told me, 'but we've learnt to be patient, and these ugly ducklings often turn into the most beautiful wines of all.' The Hasselbachs make Riesling wines in all styles from bone-dry (Trocken) up to intensely luscious Beerenauslese dessert wines.

*

LOUIS GUNTRUM

> Weingut Louis Guntrum, Rheinallee 62, 6505 Nierstein
>
> Estate bottled   47 acres of Riesling
>
> 180,000 bottles of Riesling per year
>
> Quality: 🍇🍇🍇   Price: ★★ – ★★★★
>
> Best vintages: '71, '76, '79, '83, '85, '88, '89

Hans-Joachim Louis, or 'Hajo', Guntrum has been one of the most active promoters of fine German wines internationally during the last five years. In 1987 he founded Vintners' Pride of Germany, a group of estates which market their wines jointly and work to improve the image of fine German wines. They have been an instrumental force in bringing the Riesling revival to Britain, and must be greatly thanked for this work.

'Hajo' Guntrum's estate is one of the most reliable producers of Riesling wines in Rheinhessen. He maintains a consistently high standard. The Guntrum Classic collection launched in the spring of 1987 is of an even higher quality, the Oppenheimer Sackträger wines in the traditional style being rich and succulent, and the Niersteiner Auflangen wines in the dry (Trocken) style, full, firm, and minerally. They are typical examples of the estate's style – wines which show well from shortly after bottling, but with the potential to mature in bottle for many years.

HEYL ZU HERRNSHEIM

> Weingut Freiherr Heyl zu Herrnsheim, Langgasse 3, 6505 Nierstein
>
> Estate bottled   46.5 acres of Riesling
>
> 160,000 bottles of Riesling per year
>
> Quality: 🍇🍇🍇🍇🍇   Price: ★★★ – ★★★★
>
> Best vintages: '71, '75, '76, '79, '83, '85, '86, '88, '90

None of the other great Riesling producers on the Rhine has maintained such a remarkably consistent high standard as the estate of Heyl zu Herrnsheim in Nierstein. In May 1988 estate owners Peter and Isa von Weymarn staged a vertical tasting of Riesling wines from their monopole vineyard site Niersteiner Brudersberg which proved just how long their estate has been at the top. Almost every vintage from 1945 onwards was represented, including 'disastrous' vintages such as 1956 and 1965, and virtually every wine was superb. In Germany, only the estate of Joh. Jos. Prüm on the Middle Mosel can match this.

Today the majority of the Heyl estate's wines are vinified in drier styles, and with great success. These are some of the most concentrated and supple dry Rieslings from any of the Rhine regions, though they are a shade tarter than those from the top producers of the Rheinpfalz. For non-German palates the harmoniously dry (Halbtrocken) wines will probably be the most appealing of these. The estate also makes remarkably fine traditional-style Rieslings with a touch of unfermented sweetness from the Brudersberg and Oelberg sites in Nierstein. They are by no means sweet in taste and have a complex minerally richness, the Brudersberg wines always showing greater depth and elegance.

Since the early eighties the von Weymarns have steadily been converting their vineyards over to organic cultivation. They produce the finest organic wines in Germany. The Heyl wines from their conventionally cultivated vineyards are marketed under a blue label depicting a monk, while the organic wines are marketed under a florid heraldic label.

BÜRGERMEISTER CARL KOCH ERBEN

Weingut Bürgermeister Carl Koch Erben, Wormser Strasse
62, 6504 Oppenheim

Estate bottled   11 acres of Riesling

40,000 bottles of Riesling per year

Quality: 🍇🍇🍇   Price: ★★ – ★★★

Best vintages: '71, '76, '79, '83, '86, '88, '89

Carl, or Charlie, Koch is the best wine-maker in the village of
Oppenheim. His Rieslings from the village's Kreuz and Sackträger sites are classic examples of the firm, richly fruity character typical of Oppenheim wines. Here the heavy soils and warm
micro-climate make for big, ripe wines whose mouth-filling
fruit masks a firm structure. Because of this structure the Sackträger Rieslings in particular are slow developers. Although
they can be appealing after their release onto the market, they
show their true class only after two or three years in the bottle.

Charlie Koch's Riesling wines are made the traditional way
in wooden casks, and there is no rush to bottle them or bring
them onto the estate's price list. The Kochs begin selling their
better Riesling wines only when they are two years old, though
increasing demand is already making it difficult to stick to this
policy. I sense that Charlie doesn't feel at all at home selling his
wines, and is happy to leave this task to his canny mother. He is
in his element down in the extensive cellars which lie beneath
the Kochs' ancient home, which dates back to the early Middle
Ages and has something of the air of a fairy-tale castle about it.

GEORG ALBRECHT SCHNEIDER

Weingut Georg Albrecht Schneider, Oberdorfstrasse 11,
6505 Nierstein

Estate bottled   15 acres of Riesling

53,000 bottles of Riesling per year

Quality: 🍇🍇🍇   Price: ★★ – ★★★

Best vintages: '75, '76, '79, '83, '85, '88, '89, '90

Albrecht Schneider is one of Rheinhessen's most talented wine-makers, but describes himself as 'a hopeless salesman'. It is hard to imagine this tall, lean, slightly nervous and shy figure promoting his wines in the normal manner. He gives you the impression that he would much prefer to let them speak for themselves. For this reason his excellent estate in Nierstein is only now beginning to make a name for itself, though Schneider has made impressive wines for more than a decade. What sets the wines apart from those of the other good Riesling producers in the town is their remarkable depth of flavour and 'spritz' of carbon dioxide. The estate's best Riesling wines are from the Hipping and Oelberg sites, the former firm and racy, the latter very rich, earthy, and full.

VILLA SACHSEN

Weingut Villa Sachsen, Mainzer Strasse 184, 6530 Bingen

Estate bottled   48 acres of Riesling

100,000 bottles of Riesling per year

Quality: 🍇🍇🍇   Price: ★★★ – ★★★★

Best vintages: '71, '75, '76, '79, '83, '85, '86, '88, '89

The Villa Sachsen estate is the largest owner of top-class Riesling vineyards in the north-western corner of Rheinhessen, close to the town of Bingen. Although owned by a multi-national corporation, Nestlé, the estate is run with the aim of producing high-quality wines. The yields are low and the wine-making conservative. A tasting of the estate's wines in the capacious cellars beneath the early nineteenth-century classical-style Villa Sachsen is always exciting. However, retasting the wines after they have been bottled has often been a slightly disappointing experience, for they sometimes seemed to have been rounded off before bottling to make them just a little bit more immediately attractive. The result is a loss of some of the piquant, earthy character which makes the most successful wines from the estate so impressive. The estate quite regularly makes Riesling Beerenauslese and Trockenbeerenauslese dessert wines in small quantities. These are very rich and lusciously sweet.

Rheinpfalz

Total vineyard area: 56,000 acres

Vineyard area planted with Riesling: 17%/10,000 acres

Average annual Riesling production: 40,000,000 bottles

The Rheinpfalz has the second largest acreage of Riesling vineyards in Germany behind the Mosel–Saar–Ruwer, with more than 50 per cent more Riesling acreage than the Rheingau. It isn't only in volume that the Rheinpfalz has overtaken the Rheingau, however, for there are also far more first-class Riesling producers here than in the Rheingau, and good-quality Riesling wines from the Rheinpfalz are much better value for money than those from its more famous competitor to the north. Furthermore, the Rheingau has undertaken a lot of professional promotion to create a reputation for fine dry white wines.

The Rheinpfalz, whose vineyards lie on gentle slopes immediately to the east of the Haardt mountains, is blessed with an exceptionally favourable climate. Precipitation here is relatively low, as the area lies in the rain shadow of the Haardt, which also protects it from wind, and frost flows out of the better vineyards down towards the Rhine to the east. Naturally within this picture there are considerable variations. The most climatically favoured part of the region is the stretch from Kallstadt, just north of Bad Dürkheim, south to the town of Neustadt, which is the heart of the Middle Haardt area. To the north and to the south of this there are only isolated areas with a comparably favoured micro-climate.

Here Riesling grapes will ripen fully almost every year, and dry wines with 11.5° to 12.5° of natural alcohol can regularly be made. Unlike many Alsace Riesling wines they don't taste alcoholic, because of the German tradition of not chaptalizing the better wines (adding sugar to build up their alcohol content), and because the wines have an elegant, ripe acidity which accentuates their fruitiness. As the region's wine-makers have been rediscovering the excellent possibilities for making harmonious dry Riesling wines which the local climate offers, the production of traditional-style Riesling wines (with some sweetness) has been steadily reduced during the last years.

Rheinpfalz Riesling wines don't just have more body and weight than the Rieslings from the other German regions, they also have a more extrovert fruitiness and far more aroma. In ripe vintages this can become a luscious tropical-fruit character, often combined with a tang of grapefruit. One group of Riesling producers in the region, led by estates such as Müller-Catoir and Lingenfelder, seek to accentuate this character as much as possible. Another group of producers, led by the famous estates of Dr Bürklin-Wolf and von Buhl, look towards the Rheingau as their ideal, and aim at producing clean, elegant wines that are not overpoweringly aromatic. Which approach is right is a question of personal taste, though I have to say that I think it would be extremely sad if the Riesling wines from all the Rhine regions tasted very similar.

BASSERMANN-JORDAN

Geheimer Rat Dr v. Bassermann-Jordan'sches Weingut, 6705 Deidesheim

Estate bottled   120 acres of Riesling

360,000 bottles of Riesling per year

Quality: 🍷🍷🍷🍷🍷   Price: ★★★ – ★★★★★

Best vintages: '71, '76, '79, '86, '88, '89, '90

Of the larger Riesling producers in the Rheinpfalz there can be no doubt that today Dr Ludwig von Bassermann-Jordan's estate in Deidesheim is making the finest wines. He is totally committed to Riesling, and the estate markets only Riesling wines, which are made by extremely conservative methods in wooden barrels. Not surprisingly they are absolutely classic Rheinpfalz Rieslings, aromatic, with full, ripe, slightly exotic fruit and elegant acidity. In their youth they are extremely forthcoming, yet also really refined. They age beautifully, becoming more and more classical with every year in the bottle.

Dr Ludwig von Bassermann-Jordan is one of the great gentlemen of the German wine scene, always the last to push his own wines, and always a generous and gracious host. His father was Germany's greatest wine historian, and the estate's cellars are littered with displays of Roman amphoras. A small bottle in a display cabinet in the drawing-room is the oldest wine in the world (also Roman). Many of these artifacts were discovered during vineyard cultivation in the area, whose vineyards were first planted during the late Roman period.

Since the middle of the eighties the estate has marketed all its dry Riesling wines under an Art Nouveau label. They are very fruity and harmonious, with much more character and pure fruit than the majority of dry German Rieslings. The estate's traditional-style Riesling wines are rarely sweeter than off-dry, with a juicy fruitiness, fine balance, and long aftertaste. Their label bears the family's coat of arms.

REICHSRAT VON BUHL

Weingut Reichsrat von Buhl, Weinstrasse 16–24, 6705 Deidesheim

Estate bottled   113.5 acres of Riesling

> 400,000 bottles of Riesling per year
>
> Quality: 🍇🍇🍇   Price: ★★★ – ★★★★
>
> Best vintages: '71, '75, '76, '77, '79, '81, '85, '89, '90

The famous von Buhl estate in Deidesheim has been through some ups and downs during the eighties under three different directors and three different wine-makers. In 1989 it looked as if owner Georg Enoch Buhl Reichsfreiherr von und zu Guttenberg would mothball the entire estate and lease out its vineyards in a piecemeal fashion to other growers in the area. Thankfully the prospect of the estate ceasing to exist in the form it has had for more than 140 years was averted when a Japanese consortium backed by the electronics giant Sanyo took out a twelve-year-plus lease on the estate.

They face a number of major problems in rebuilding the estate's name as one of the premier producers of Riesling wines in the Rheinpfalz. The most basic of these is the style of the wine-making. In good vintages which bring ripe grapes, von Buhl continues to produce high-class wines, particularly from the great vineyards of neighbouring Forst–Ungeheuer, Freundstück, Jesuitengarten, and Kirchenstück – but in lesser vintages the wines are hard and angular, and lack the juicy fruitiness which is the hallmark of fine Rheinpfalz Riesling wines.

DR BÜRKLIN-WOLF

> Weingut Dr Bürklin-Wolf, 6706 Wachenheim
>
> Estate bottled   193 acres of Riesling
>
> 840,000 bottles of Riesling per year
>
> Quality: 🍇🍇🍇🍇   Price: ★★★ – ★★★★★
>
> Best vintages: '71, '75, '76, '79, '83, '85, '86, '89, '90

The Bürklin-Wolf estate is one of the most important wine estates of Germany, both in terms of reputation and the scale of its quality wine production. Given this scale, the quality of the regular wines is very good. The huge area of Riesling vineyards at the estate's disposal also enables them regularly to adopt strict selective harvesting in a way which small estates cannot. The top-quality Riesling Auslese, Beerenauslese and Trockenbeerenauslese wines which result are often among the best in the region. The wine-making at the estate has been a little up and down during recent years, though.

The history of the Bürklin family in Wachenheim goes back almost four hundred years, and that of the Wolf family more than two hundred. Both were important vineyard owners, and when they came together in 1875 a great estate was born. For more than a century Dr Albert Bürklin and his son of the same name ran the estate with uncompromising professionalism. Today the estate is owned by the second Dr Albert-Bürklin's daughter Bettina, who runs it together with director Herr Raquet. The estate's enormous cellars lie under the Kolb Hof in the middle of Wachenheim. Here wooden casks stand beside rows of stainless-steel tanks, a clear expression of the estate's wine-making style, of what George Raquet calls 'a symbiosis of tradition and modernity'.

In the spring of 1987 the estate launched their Selection Geheimrat Dr Albert-Bürklin, a luxury range of dry Rieslings from their top vineyard sites in Wachenheim and Ruppertsberg.

KOEHLER-RUPRECHT

Weingut Koehler-Ruprecht, Weinstrasse 84, 6701 Kallstadt

Estate bottled   13.5 acres of Riesling

50,000 bottles of Riesling per year

Quality: 🍇🍇🍇🍇🍇   Price: ★★★ – ★★★★★

Best vintages: '71, '73, '76, '79, '81, '83, '85, '86, '88, '89

Bernd Philippi, owner and wine-maker of Koehler-Ruprecht, produces the greatest dry Riesling wines in the Rheinpfalz and perhaps in the whole of Germany. They have such a power and concentration that only the very best dry Rieslings from Alsace and the Wachau in Austria can match them. Bernd could hardly be more nonchalant about this though, so that you feel it was never a great struggle to produce these sensational wines, but rather something which happened by itself while he was having fun with wine.

Bernd Philippi is the embodiment of *joie de vivre*, living, eating, and drinking life to the full. However, a quick glance round the estate's capacious new cellars is enough to convince that a very considerable amount of work has been done here recently. Here all the Koehler-Ruprecht wines are matured in old wooden casks for a period of up to two years, and the dry wines are made just as Bernd's father and grandfather made them.

The estate's Rieslings in the sweeter style are hardly less fine, and are always balanced so that they taste just off-dry. Like the dry wines they are brimming with fruit and show the exotic overtones in the bouquet so typical of the region's Rieslings. All the estate's wines benefit from at least three or four years' maturation in the bottle before drinking, and should ideally have a full decade. In vintages when the right conditions occur botrytis-affected grapes are selectively harvested to make extremely powerful and unctuous dessert wines.

LINGENFELDER

Weingut Lingenfelder, Hauptstrasse 27, 6711 Grosskarlbach

Estate bottled   7 acres of Riesling

18,000 bottles of Riesling per year

Quality: 🍇🍇🍇🍇🍇   Price: ★★★ – ★★★★

Best vintages: '71, '76, '79, '83, '88, '89

Rainer Lingenfelder is one of the Rheinpfalz's most fervent proponents of the region's classic style of Riesling wines. In spite of having worked and studied in Bordeaux and various wine-producing regions in California, Australia, New Zealand

and Egypt, he has not become an internationalist. The idea of producing some kind of anonymous international-style white wine that spurns the traditions of his region strikes Rainer as being the kiss of death. For him there can be no compromise in the vineyards or the cellar. The estate's Riesling vineyards are stocked exclusively with the low-yielding Rheinpfalz clone N90, which many modernistic wine producers in the region regard as too aromatic. In the cellar minimal handling means just that, the only treatment which the wines receive before bottling being a light filtration.

The Lingenfelder Rieslings come as a shock to many people who have grown up with the idea that German Riesling is a light, flowery, quaffing wine. Even in lesser vintages these are big, powerful wines packed with fruit, and have a bouquet that can knock you down at twenty yards. The dry (Trocken) Rieslings have these characteristics most strongly. After a couple of years in the bottle they have a similar balance to medium-bodied white Burgundies, but with a crisper finish. The traditional-style wines have little sweetness, tasting succulently fruity and off-dry. In both styles they have a wonderful exotic grapefruity character.

Whenever there is a significant amount of botrytis-affected grapes in the vineyard, Rainer selectively harvests these to make rich Auslese, Beerenauslese, or Trockenbeerenauslese dessert wines. These are encouraged to ferment as far as possible so that they achieve higher alcohol levels and less sweetness than is typical for Germany.

GEORG MOSSBACHER

Weingut Georg Mossbacher, Hauptstrasse 27, 6701 Forst

Estate bottled   18 acres of Riesling

68,000 bottles of Riesling per year

Quality: 🍇🍇🍇🍇   Price: ★★★

Best vintages: '71, '76, '79, '81, '83, '86, '88, '89

Richard Mossbacher makes the finest Riesling wines from the vineyards of the famous wine village of Forst. As a result of a strict policy of declassifying his wines to lower-quality designations, his Riesling Kabinett wines have a fullness of body and richness of fruit that make the Riesling Kabinetts from many other good producers in the region look pretty thin and characterless. Richard Mossbacher, who is a reserved middle-aged man with white hair, couldn't be more modest about his exceptional wines. After getting to know him, though, you realize that he indeed knows just how good his wines are. Behind the modest front is a wine-maker of the highest professionalism.

There is nothing showy about the Mossbacher estate either. The small group of buildings at the southern end of the cobbled main street of Forst looks completely unexceptional. Truly exceptional are Georg Mossbacher's Riesling Auslese, Beerenauslese, and Trockenbeerenauslese dessert wines. They are nothing short of sensational: perfect marriages of enormous concentration of flavour with great finesse.

MÜLLER-CATOIR

Weingut Müller-Catoir, 6730 Neustadt–Haardt

Estate bottled   14.5 acres of Riesling

54,000 bottles of Riesling per year

Quality: 🍇🍇🍇🍇   Price: ★★★ – ★★★★

Best vintages: '71, '76, '79, '81, '83, '85, '88, '89

What makes Hans-Günter Schwarz one of Germany's greatest wine-makers is not only the superb wine he has been making at the Müller-Catoir estate for two decades, but the guiding influence he has had on many of the young generation of wine-makers in the Rheinpfalz. At Müller-Catoir Herr Schwarz's greatest achievements are undoubtedly the outstanding wines he has made from the Scheurebe, Rieslaner, and Muskateller grape varieties. However, the estate's drier-style Riesling wines are also impressive. They are full-throttle Rheinpfalz Riesling wines with a powerful, extrovert bouquet of grapefruit and tropical fruits. Vividly fruity and 'spritzy' with carbon dioxide in their youth, they mature to a mouth-filling mellow fullness after four or more years in the bottle.

In contrast to Hans-Günter Schwarz's jovial directness, estate owner Heinrich Catoir has a somewhat aristocratic air about him, which seems befitting in the imposing nineteenth-century Catoir mansion. However, neither makes any great secret of how they achieve the estate's extremely high quality level. The vineyard work is orientated towards achieving a low yield of fully ripe grapes, which are picked very late for optimum ripeness. In the cellar the wines are pumped and filtered as little as possible and there is no fining of either the grape juice or the wine.

PFEFFINGEN

Weingut Pfeffingen, Fuhrmann-Eymael, 6702 Bad Dürkheim

Estate bottled   19 acres of Riesling

72,000 bottles of Riesling per year

Quality: ᵱᵱᵱᵱᵱ   Price: ★★★ – ★★★★★

Best vintages: '71, '73, '75, '76, '79, '81, '83, '85, '88, '89, '90

Just as Koehler-Ruprecht are the star producers of dry Riesling wines in the Rheinpfalz, so Karl Fuhrmann, with his son-in-law Günter Eymael and daughter Doris Eymael, are the star producers of sweeter-style Riesling wines in the region. Those in the traditional and medium-dry Halbtrocken styles have a brilliance, intense fruitiness, and elegance which has to be tasted to be believed. Year in year out their wines stand out even among those of the region's other top estates.

The special character of this estate's wines is the result of the excellent vineyards of Ungstein, and a mixture of Rheinpfalz and Mosel wine-making skills. Karl Fuhrmann began building up the Pfeffingen estate in 1952. From the 1980 vintage onwards his skills have been complemented by those of Günter Eymael, a member of the Eymael family from Ürzig on the Middle Mosel. He has brought the light touch of the Mosel to the estate's Riesling wines, giving them a remarkable delicacy and subtlety for Rieslings from this far south.

The fabulous Riesling dessert wines from this estate are among the greatest wines made in this style anywhere in the world: extremely concentrated, luscious, and complex in flavour and bouquet. Sadly they are great rarities, the estate owners preferring to make dessert wines from the Scheurebe variety.

KARL SCHAEFER

Weingut Karl Schaefer, Weinstrasse Sud 30, 6702 Bad Dürkheim

Estate bottled   33 acres of Riesling

160,000 bottles of Riesling per year

Quality: 🍇🍇🍇🍇   Price: ★★★ – ★★★★

Best vintages: '71, '76, '79, '81, '83, '85, '86, '89, '90

The Karl Schaefer estate, which is owned by Dr Wolf Fleischmann and directed by his step-son Bernhard Lehmeyer, has long been one of the most reliable producers of Riesling wines in the Mittelhaardt area of the Rheinpfalz. Most impressive of all are their dry (Trocken) Rieslings, which are extremely fine and elegant. Their forthright fruitiness makes them very appealing, beautifully balancing their fruity acidity. Every vintage, whether 'good' or 'poor', the Schaefer Riesling wines are simply delicious.

It is difficult to work out what the secret of the Schaefer estate's excellence is, though the main principle is 'hands off'. The wine-making for the traditional-style (with some sweetness) wines is 'Mosel' style, the wines always retaining a spritz of carbon dioxide and an extremely fruity sweetness. No concessions to gimmicky wine-making or marketing are made here.

WEGELER-DEINHARD

Gutsverwaltung Wegeler-Deinhard, Weinstrasse 10, 6705 Deidesheim

Estate bottled   31.5 acres of Riesling

102,000 bottles of Riesling per year

Quality: 🍇🍇🍇   Price: ★★★ – ★★★★

Best vintages: '71, '76, '79, '81, '85, '86, '88, '89

Although Deinhard's estate in the Rheingau is generally acknowledged to be the best of their three estates, my personal vote would go to their estate in Deidesheim, where Heinz Bauer makes beautifully clean, fruity Rheinpfalz Rieslings. Of these it is the late-harvested Spätlese and Auslese quality wines from the Forster Ungeheuer site which most impress. They have a rich almost chewy pineappley fruit, lots of substance, and a firm finish. They age magnificently, and often don't show their best until they have been in the bottle for three or four years. In comparison, the Riesling wines from the Deidesheimer Herrgottsacker and Ruppertsberger Linsenbusch sites are rather more straightforward, although elegant.

The dry wines from the estate have come on in leaps and bounds during the last decade, and the traditional-style wines are very well balanced. Heinz Bauer also makes the wines for the Dr Deinhard estate which shares the same cellar, but whose wines are rarely exported.

WERLÉ

Weingut Otto Werlé, Altes Schlössel, 6701 Forst

Estate bottled   26.5 acres of Riesling

72,000 bottles of Riesling per year

Quality: 🍇🍇🍇   Price: ★★★ – ★★★★

Best vintages: '71, '76, '79, '86, '88, '89, '90

Hardy and Claus Werlé run one of the most traditional wine

estates in the Rheinpfalz. Little has changed here during the decades since the last war. The vineyards are still cultivated without the use of modern fertilizers and sprays (in effect, fully organic viticulture), and all the wines are left to ferment as they wish. As a result very few are sweeter than off-dry. The estate's policy is to sell only bone-dry Rieslings as dry (Trocken) wines, and to market everything else as being in the conventional style, though they are much drier than the great majority of wines sold as such.

The philosophy of the Werlés seems to grow out of the sixteenth-century mansion house in the centre of Forst. The virginia creeper covered walls of its spacious courtyard exude an almost medieval atmosphere. In spite of this, the Werlé wines don't taste rustic or woody, but rather fruity, firm and minerally.

Württemberg

Total vineyard area: 23,750 acres

Vineyard area planted with Riesling: 25%/5,190 acres

Average annual Riesling production: 25,000,000 bottles

Considering how many acres are planted with the Riesling vine in Württemberg, its wines of this variety are remarkably unknown. If the region is associated with any wines outside the state of Baden-Württemberg, it is with pale-coloured red wines. In fact Württemberg's top growers are now producing some impressive Riesling wines, and one of the reasons why they are little known is probably the heavy wine consumption of the chauvinistic Württembergers.

The region's generally heavy soils and warm summers make for full-bodied Rieslings which are much softer than those of any other of Germany's wine-producing regions. In contrast to the country's most northerly regions, where the wine-growers work and work to achieve ripeness in the grapes at all costs, here they have to work carefully in the vineyard and cellar to retain freshness. The region's best Rieslings are almost invariably dry wines, full-bodied, with a mellow fruitiness and modest acidity. They are good food wines, particularly for meat dishes with lightly spiced sauces, sausage, and semi-hard French cheeses.

GRAF ADELMANN

Weingut Graf Adelmann, Burg Schaubeck, 7141 Kleinbottwar

Estate bottled   9.5 acres of Riesling

30,000 bottles of Riesling per year

Quality: 🍇🍇🍇🍇   Price: ★★★ – ★★★★

Best vintages: '79, '83, '85, '86, '89, '90

Michael Graf Adelmann is one of the most charming of all Germany's top estate owners. Giving an impression of somewhat indefinite age, or rather youthfulness, he is aristocratic without in any way being stiff or overbearing. His greatest wines are undoubtedly his new oak-aged red wines from the Lemberger, Clevner, and Samtrot varieties (which are found almost only in this region). His dry Rieslings can also be impressive, though, with a full, lemony-exotic character and enough acidity not to be fat or too broad. The best come from the Kleinbottwarer Süssmund vineyard site, though what stands out most strongly from the label is not the name of the vineyard or even of the estate, but the name 'Brussele' or 'Brussele'r Spitze' under which the estate's wines have been sold since the last century. The 'Brussele' label is elegant and modern in spite of bearing the Adelmann coat of arms, and the 'Brussele'r Spitze' label under which the top wines are marketed is baroquely traditional.

The Adelmann estate is one of the few in the region to produce Auslese and Eiswein dessert wines from Riesling when conditions permit, as they do occasionally. These are extremely rich, luscious wines that need many years to reach their peak.

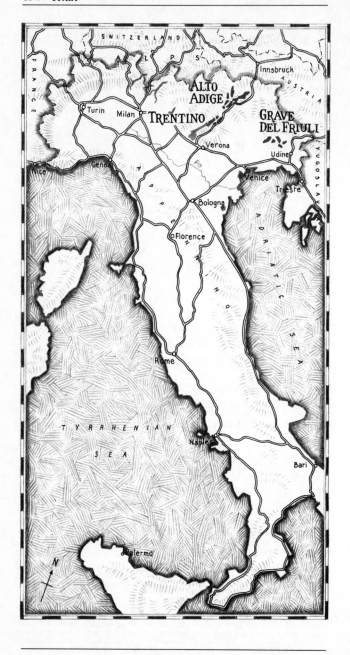

ITALY

Total vineyard area: 2,800,000 acres
Vineyard area planted with Riesling: less than 1%/200 acres
Average annual Riesling production:

Italy is the world's largest wine producer, averaging 10,000,000,000 bottles per year, of which the Italians themselves drink nearly two thirds. Of the hundreds of native grape varieties planted in the widely scattered wine-producing regions of Italy that stretch from the island of Pantelleria off the African coast to the lower slopes of the Alps in Süd Tirol/Alto Adige more than 700 miles to the north, Riesling Italico is one of the more important. While Riesling Italico produces some very pleasant wines in both Italy and Austria, none of these can be compared with the finest wines produced from the true Riesling vine.

In Italy true white Riesling is known as Riesling Renano, and is produced in significant quantities as a varietal wine only in the provinces of Trentino-Alto Adige, Friuli–Venezia Giulia, and Veneto. However, even in these areas Riesling is something of a rarity. In Süd Tirol/Alto Adige there are a mere 112 acres of the variety, for example, and though the areas planted with Riesling in Trentino and Friuli are considerably larger the variety is still only of minor importance there. Invariably vinified as a medium-bodied dry wine, Italian Rieslings are usually very clean, crisp, and quite fruity. However, they are rarely anything more than this. In general, the white wines made from Pinot Grigio (Pinot Gris), Chardonnay, and Tocai in northwest Italy are more characterful and interesting than those made from Riesling Renano.

JERMANN

Vignaioli Jermann, Via Monte Fortino 17, 34070 Villanova
di Farra

Estate bottled   7.5 acres of Riesling

10,000 bottles of Riesling per year

Quality: 🍇🍇🍇   Price: ★★★

Best vintages: '85, '86, '88, '90

Silvio Jermann is one of the young star wine-makers of Friuli.
After studying at the wine schools of Conegliano and San
Michele he began working at the family business in 1974, but
his desire to modernize the estate and make a cleaner more
forthrightly fruity style of dry white wine than his father,
Angelo, led to bitter disagreements. In 1977 he left for Canada
to work as a wine consultant. In his absence his father found
that the innovations which Silvio had already made in the cellar
resulted in wines which sold very well, and slowly the rift
between them was healed. After more than a year oscillating
between Canada and Italy, Silvio returned to Friuli and began
making the wines he had been dreaming of since his studies in
the sixties.

His Riesling Renano hasn't attracted as much attention as
some of his other wines, but it is one of the best of the varietal
white wines which he makes. Primrose yellow in colour (from
macerating the crushed grapes on their skins before pressing), it
has a full, quite spicy bouquet of peach and melon. With 12° of
natural alcohol it is full-bodied and lushly fruit, with a touch of
bitterness at the finish. For Riesling it is a big, extrovert mouthful, but its power and richness is matched by crispness enough
to balance. It is an ideal wine to drink with quite strongly
flavoured spicy food, and is at its best when young and vividly
fresh.

LUXEMBOURG

Total vineyard area: 3,250 acres

Vineyard area planted with Riesling: 10%/350 acres

Average annual Riesling production: 1,500,000 bottles

Principally because it is so small and because the chauvinistic Luxembourgers drink the great majority of the Grand Duchy's wine production themselves, internationally Luxembourg wines are virtually unknown. This is unfortunate, for though the dry Riesling wines produced here fail to reach the heights which the best Alsatian and Austrian dry Rieslings do, they can none the less be very good wines indeed. What makes this position particularly sad is that the dry Riesling wines of Luxembourg are in tune with international taste, and would undoubtedly find markets outside the Grand Duchy given the right kind of promotion.

Although the vineyards of Luxembourg lie in the Mosel valley immediately to the west of the German wine-growing region of Mosel–Saar–Ruwer, the wines they produce are completely different from those made just across the border in Germany. This is the result of different soils and different wine-making traditions. The great majority of vineyards in the Mosel–Saar–Ruwer have shallow slate soils, while those in Luxembourg have deep limestone soils. Like the vineyards in the German part of the Mosel valley, those in Luxembourg are also planted on sloping ground facing south or south-west. In Luxembourg, though, the landscape is more gentle and rounded than the often precipitous slopes and ragged escarpments of the Mosel.

In Germany the tradition is for very low-alcohol wines which often have a slight sweetness, whereas Luxembourg wine-makers have traditionally added sugar to their fermenting wines in order to increase their alcoholic content (chaptalization), and fermented them to bone-dryness. The result is that Luxembourg Riesling wines are always bone-dry, medium-bodied (just over 11° of alcohol), with a crisp acidity. The best have a very clean appley-lemony fruitiness, with overtones of peach and exotic fruits.

CLOS DES ROCHERS

Clos des Rochers, Bernard-Massard, 8 rue du Pont, 6773 Gravenmacher

Estate bottled   7.5 acres of Riesling

32,000 bottles of Riesling per year

Quality: 🍇🍇🍇   Price: ★★★

Best vintages: '83, '85, '88, '89

The history of the Clos des Rochers estate goes back a long way before the foundation of the Bernard-Massard sparkling wine group, of which it is now a part (though the Clasen family remain owners of the vineyards). The Clos des Rochers wines are some of the freshest and the most refined Rieslings produced in Luxembourg. Even in lesser vintages, they have a bouquet of ripe apples and quince that leaps out of the glass at you. In the best vintages the aromas are more peachy with subtle exotic fruit overtones. Dry and racy, they have a finely nuanced fruitiness on the palate. Unusually for Luxembourg, Hubert Clasen makes his wines to last, and though they are very attractive in their youth they will all keep a good decade.

MME ALY DUHR ET FILS

Domaine Mme Aly Duhr et Fils, 9 rue Aly Duhr, 5401 Ahn

Estate bottled   4 acres of Riesling

18,000 bottles of Riesling per year

Quality: 🍇🍇🍇   Price: ★★★
Best vintages: '83, '85, '86, '88, '90

There is a handful of really impressive Riesling wine producers in Luxembourg, of which the Duhr family are amongst the best, consistently producing wines with more depth and structure than most of their competitors. The estate is certainly the most dynamic in the Grand Duchy, having produced the region's first new oak-aged white wine in 1982, and the region's first red wine in 1988. The estate's wines are made by Leon Duhr under the guidance of his brother Abi Duhr, who also works as a wine merchant in Luxembourg. Their wines were always impressive, but since 1987 they have implemented a strict policy of yield reduction in their vineyards which has given them an extra degree of intensity. Genial as they are, the Duhr brothers leave you in no doubt that their ambition is to make wines of a quality hitherto unknown in Luxembourg.

The Aly Duhr Riesling wines are medium-bodied and can seem a little firm and unyielding in their youth. They need one to two years in the bottle to open up and show their real class. Then they are racy wines, packed with appley, peachy, and citrusy fruit. The wines of recent vintages have the potential to mature for a decade or more in the bottle. Their best Riesling wines are sold under the shockingly modern black and yellow label of the Domaines et Tradition association of Luxembourg wine estates, of which they are founder members.

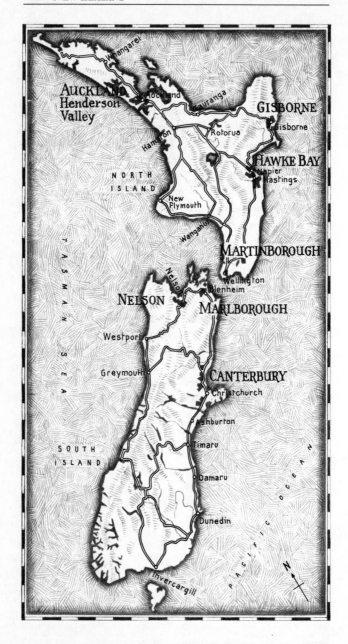

AUCKLAND
Henderson
Valley

Whangarei

Auckland

Tauranga

GISBORNE

Gisborne

Rotorua

NORTH
ISLAND

HAWKE BAY
Napier
Hastings

Hamilton

New
Plymouth

Wangahui

MARTINBOROUGH

TASMAN SEA

Nelson

Wellington
Blenheim

NELSON

MARLBOROUGH

Westport

Greymouth

CANTERBURY

Christchurch

Ashburton

SOUTH
ISLAND

Timaru

Oamaru

Dunedin

PACIFIC OCEAN

Invercargill

N

NEW ZEALAND

Total vineyard area: 10,470 acres
Vineyard area planted with Riesling: 6%/635 acres
Average annual Riesling production: 3,000,000 bottles

Riesling is far from being the most important grape variety in New Zealand, where Müller-Thurgau (3,000 acres) and Chardonnay (1,000 acres and rising fast) are easily the dominant white-grape varieties. However, New Zealand produces some of the finest Riesling wines in the New World. This is undoubtedly the result of the country's cool maritime climate, which makes for a long ripening season. Unlike some other New World countries, New Zealand successfully markets Riesling domestically, as Paul Treacher, Managing Director of the giant Corbans wine group, told me: 'Rhine Riesling wines used to have problems on the market because cheap Müller-Thurgau wines were sold as "Riesling-Sylvaner". Now that most of the Müller-Thurgau goes into bag-in-box, Rhine Riesling has emerged as a premium varietal.'

New Zealand Riesling wines are nothing like their dry, full-bodied, and often rather alcoholic cousins from Australia. Instead, they are off-dry, clean and crisp, with an appealing balance of ripe acidity and juicy fruitiness. In many ways they are comparable with drier-style Riesling wines from the more southerly regions of Germany, or lighter Alsace Rieslings. The most impressive currently being made in New Zealand are the dessert wines produced by a handful of growers from botrytis-affected grapes. If not quite in the same class as the finest wines made in this style in Germany and Alsace, they are none the less far more exciting than the majority of dessert Rieslings from Australia or North America.

Considering that the first Riesling grapes in New Zealand were harvested in 1975 the present quality level is quite an achievement. Given that New Zealand wine-makers have been concentrating their efforts on fine-tuning their already impressive Sauvignon Blanc and Chardonnay white wines, rather than on perfecting their Riesling wine-making, it is even more remarkable. The most successful wines produced so far indicate that with more commitment to the variety New Zealand's wine-makers can produce Rieslings every bit as good as the Sauvignons and Chardonnay wines which have been so highly praised by the wine press during the last few years. In Marlborough, at the northern tip of the South Island, the combination of a genuinely cool climate and a stony soil looks particularly promising for the production of fine Riesling wines.

If there is a problem with wine-making in New Zealand it is that wine-makers hungry for international recognition tend to transplant techniques which have been successful elsewhere wholesale onto their very different grapes. The favourite model is, not surprisingly, nearby Australia. It is to be hoped that New Zealander wine-makers will gain enough confidence to realize that they don't need to try to reproduce the more showy style of Australian wine. The best New Zealand wines have wonderfully pure, crisp fruit flavours, and are more elegant than almost any other New World white wines. This is something special, which deserves highlighting, rather than burying under heavy new oak and yeast flavours.

Marlborough

Total vineyard area: 2,775 acres

Vineyard area planted with Riesling: 11.5%/320 acres

Average annual Riesling production: 1,500,000 bottles

In contrast to the other New Zealand wine-producing regions, where Riesling plays a comparatively minor role, Marlborough deserves some detailed description. Just over half the Riesling vineyards in New Zealand are here, only here does the vine variety account for a significant proportion of vineyard plantations, and of all the New Zealand wine-producing regions it has the greatest potential to produce high-quality Riesling wines.

The Marlborough vineyards are situated at the northern tip of the South Island on the broad alluvial plains of the Wairau River just before it flows into the Cook Strait. The climate here really is exceptional: cool, yet a little warmer than any of the classic Riesling wine-producing regions of Germany. Marlborough enjoys the highest average number of sunshine hours per year anywhere in New Zealand – 2,449, compared with 1,574 in the Mosel and 1,712 in the Rheinpfalz! The risk of heavy rains during the harvest is low, which means that the grapes can be left late on the vines to take advantage of the long, slow ripening season. Summer drought caused by drying north-westerly winds can be a problem, and most vineyards therefore have a trickle-irrigation system.

The soils range from deep alluvial silt to very shallow stony soils over deep shingle. On these less fertile soils yields are moderate, comparable with those achieved with Riesling in the classic European regions. Here, given professional vineyard management, exciting Riesling wines with both a good amount of body, full peachy fruit, and real elegance can be produced. Their elegance is the result of the high content of ripe acidity in Marlborough wines (which also enables white Chardonnay and Sauvignon Blanc wines to be produced that are high in alcohol yet neither heavy nor hot).

Given the region's many advantages it is perhaps surprising that it was only in 1973 that the first vineyards were planted here (by Montana Wines). The quality of the wines they produced at their huge Riverlands winery in the late seventies demonstrated the potential of the region, and others rushed to plant. The dramatic critical and commercial success of Cloudy Bay Winery's Sauvignon Blanc from its debut vintage in 1985

almost singlehandedly made the region's international reputation for premium-quality white wines. Riesling is only the
third most important premium grape variety here by acreage,
behind Chardonnay and Sauvignon Blanc, but as a result of the
commitment to it by a handful of important wineries it will
surely play an important role in the region's future.

DRY RIVER

Dry River Wines, Puruatanga Road, P.O. Box 72,
 Martinborough

2,000 bottles of late-harvest Riesling per year

Quality: 🍇🍇🍇🍇   Price: ★★★★

Best vintages: '87, '89, '90

Neil McCallum runs an extraordinary little winery in the town
of Martinborough at the southern tip of New Zealand's North
Island, making wines from grapes grown on his home vineyard
and from across the Cook Strait in Marlborough. Though his
winery building is only a modest wooden shed it looks remarkably stylish from the outside. This makes the Heath Robinson
style 'equipment' (much of it ex-brewery) which you find inside
all the more of a shock. In this improvised winery Neil McCallum makes wines which have not only an astonishing richness
and concentration, but also remarkable finesse. No doubt his
training as a research chemist, including a doctorate from
Oxford University, has added a wealth of useful knowledge to
his perfectionistic spirit, and this has much to do with the
quality of the wines he produces.

His late-harvested Rhine Rieslings, made from Marlborough
fruit, are classic examples of Dry River's style of wine-making.
They range from modestly sweet mid-weight wines in lesser
vintages to very rich lusciously sweet wines in the best years. All
are blessed with a scintillating interplay of racy acidity and
honeyed Riesling fruit, and a finely nuanced bouquet. It is
obvious from these wines that Neil McCallum's aim with Riesling is to match the very finest Auslese and Beerenauslese des-

sert wines produced from the variety in Germany, and already he is not far from achieving this goal.

HUNTER'S

Hunter's Wines, P.O. Box 839, Blenheim

20,000 bottles of Riesling per year

Quality: 🍇🍇🍇   Price: ★★★

Best vintages: '86, '88, '89, '90

From modest beginnings in an old cider factory in Christ-church in 1982 Hunter's Wines has become one of the most consistent producers of dry white wines in Marlborough. After founder Ernie Hunter's death in a car crash in 1987 at the age of only thirty-seven his wife, Jane, has taken over the running of the winery. From a grape-growing family in South Australia, Jane Hunter was national viticulturalist for Montana Wines until her husband's death. Her talents in vineyard management are complemented by those of wine-maker John Belsham and Australian wine-making consultant Dr Tony Jordan. Though she is less extrovert and forthright than her late husband, her charm and depth of knowledge makes her no lesser an ambas-sador for New Zealand wines.

The Hunter's Riesling wines are quite full-bodied, yet very crisp and clean in flavour. Because of their quite pronounced lemony acidity they taste dry in spite of a little touch of sweet-ness. They are fine examples of the elegant style of Riesling which Marlborough is capable of producing, and could easily be mistaken for finer dry-style wines from the south of Germany. If they had just a little more fruit they would be really first-class wines.

MATUA

Matua Valley Wines Ltd, Waikoukou Road, Waimauku, Auckland

48,000 bottles of Riesling per year

Quality: 🍇🍇🍇   Price: ★★★

Best vintages: '88, '89, '90

Ross and Bill Spence run one of the most innovative and professional family-owned wineries in New Zealand. In their
unique octagonal winery building, set above their vineyards in
the green rolling countryside of Waimauku, just north of Auckland, they make an impressive range of red and white varietal
wines. With virtually every vintage since their foundation in
1976 one or more of their wines has dramatically improved
because of changes in grape sources or wine-making. Continual
critical attention to the wine-making by Ross Spence is the
key to this. Talking to him in his laboratory, which is as well
equipped as his modern winery, you are left in no doubt
that his ambition is to be one of the leading fine-wine producers
in New Zealand.

The Matua Rhine Riesling wines made a big jump forward
with the 1988 vintage when the winery began using grapes from
Marlborough, where they have made a long-term commitment
with contract growers. Up until the 1987 vintage their Riesling
wines had been produced from Hawke's Bay fruit, and had been
pleasant, soft, and no more than reasonably fruity. The new-
style Matua Rhine Riesling wines are much crisper and more
elegant. Off-dry and of medium body, they have classic herbal
and confectionery Riesling aromas. The clean appley-peachy
fruit flavours and racy acidity give an impression of crisp
dryness.

MERLEN

Merlen Wines, P.O. Box 7, Renwick, Marlborough

15,000 bottles of Riesling per year

Quality: 🍇🍇🍇🍇   Price: ★★★

Best vintages: '88, '89, '90

Launched by Almuth Lorentz in 1987 with a highly acclaimed Chardonnay, Merlen is the newest star winery in the Marlborough region. Given her German origins, it isn't perhaps surprising that Almuth should make impressive Riesling wines as well as good Chardonnays. Her first Riesling wine, the 1988 vintage, is easily the most impressive Riesling in a non-dessert wine style that I have tasted from New Zealand. Medium-bodied and off-dry, it has bea iful crisp peachy fruit, with racy acidity and a long finish.

Almuth Lorentz made her first wines in Marlborough in 1982. While in New Zealand on a working holiday during her studies at the Geisenheim wine school in Germany she met Marlborough grape grower Ernie Hunter at a party on New Year's Eve 1981 and persuaded him he should become a wine producer. Her first vintage at Hunter's earned a clutch of medals. Now with nearly a decade in the region behind her, Almuth Lorentz is one of the most experienced wine-makers in Marlborough, though still only in her early thirties.

What makes her Riesling wines so impressive is their elegance. No doubt many other wineries in the region could achieve similar results, but at present several seem to be making the mistake of trying to produce 'big', rich Riesling wines. For Almuth Lorentz, intense, clean fruit flavours are everything. 'I want to make delicate Riesling wines,' she told me, 'wines which are a complete contrast to the powerful oaky Chardonnay white wines which I'm best known for.' This means earlier picking than most of her competitors, little skin contact (macerating the crushed grapes on their skins before pressing), and a very long cool fermentation.

STONELEIGH

Corbans Wines Ltd, 426 North Road, Henderson, Auckland 8

Estate bottled   42 acres of Riesling

120,000 bottles of Riesling per year

Quality: 🍇🍇🍇   Price: ★★★

Best vintages: '86, '89, '90

Planted in 1980, the 272-acre Stoneleigh Vineyard in Marlborough produces the Corbans group's top Riesling wine. Launched with the 1985 vintage, it is made in a bigger style than that of the smaller 'boutique' wineries in Marlborough. Though the first vintages have been a little hit-and-miss, the best wines produced so far have been off-dry, with a rich peachy-exotic fruitiness and enough acidity to make them taste lighter and cleaner than their alcohol content (between 12° and 12.5°) would lead you to expect.

The driving force behind Corbans is General Manager Paul Treacher, who despite a rather boyish appearance is a highly professional manager with a very sophisticated understanding of wine. Since he took over his present position in 1984 Corbans have gone from strength to strength, with the company placing ever more emphasis on fine-wine production. Though they are also large producers of bulk wines, some of the finest white and red wines I tasted in New Zealand were made by Corbans.

They are the work of a team of five wine-makers led by Kerry Hitchcock at Te Kauwhata, south of Auckland. I have the impression that when their wines occasionally miss the mark it is due to a lack of nerve rather than any lack of talent.

TE WHARE RA

Te Whare Ra Wines, Anglesea St, Renwick

3 acres of Riesling

3,500 bottles of late-harvest Riesling per year

7,000 bottles of other Riesling per year

LATE-HARVEST RIESLINGS

Quality: 🍇🍇🍇🍇   Price: ★★★★

OTHER RIESLINGS

Quality: 🍇   Price: ★★★

Best vintages: '85, '87, '89

Allen and Joyce Hogan are fanatics in the best sense of the word. Neither of them had any professional training in wine-making when, before Marlborough had become established as one of New Zealand's premier wine-producing regions, they became only the second winery in the region. Rhine Riesling is the only varietal wine which they have produced since their first vintage in 1982. Since 1985 they have selectively harvested botrytis-affected grapes to make luscious Riesling dessert wines. These are their best wines, and they are rightly renowned for them.

In the beginning these selected late-harvest wines were made from whatever grapes with a suitable degree of botrytis infection could be found. The 1985 Botrytis Selection was made from a mixture of Riesling and Gewürztraminer grapes, and the 1986 from Riesling, Gewürztraminer, and Müller-Thurgau grapes. Te Whare Ra now make two grades of botrytized dessert wine: the rich, sweet Botrytis Bunch Selection and the yet richer and sweeter Botrytis Berry Selection. Since the 1987 vintage these wines have been made only from Riesling grapes and have a better harmony as a result. In the pure Riesling dessert wines from Te Whare Ra the dried fruits flavours and very high sweetness are more or less balanced by the acidity.

Te Whare Ra's straight Riesling, which is marketed under the Duke of Marlborough name, is also an opulent wine. Indeed, in some vintages it seems a little overblown, with up to 12.5° alcohol, obvious sweetness, and rather soft acidity.

Other Regions

BABICH

Hawke's Bay

Babich Wines Ltd, Babich Road, Henderson, Auckland 8

12,000 bottles of Riesling per year

Quality: 🍇🍇🍇   Price: ★★★

Best vintages: '85, '86, '88, '89, '90

Joseph Babich made his first wines in 1916, planting the Babich family vineyard in Henderson in 1919. Today his two sons, Peter and Joe, run the company. Joe Babich is best known as a maker of fine Chardonnay white wines, and particularly that from the Irongate vineyard in Hawke's Bay (a superb wine). In fact the grapes for the Babich Rhine Riesling wines used to come from here too, though this was never declared on the label. They now come from a neighbouring Hawke's Bay vineyard in Fernhill, and are deliberately harvested early for a light, crisp style of wine. With about 10° of alcohol it is indeed very low in alcohol for a Hawke's Bay wine, with well-defined floral–herbal aromas and flavours. It used to be made with an obvious sweetness, but the wine is now off-dry. In fact in many vintages it tastes almost bone-dry because of its pronounced acidity. This makes it a good food wine as well as giving it the potential to age for some years in the bottle.

COLLARD BROTHERS

Collard Brothers, 303 Lincoln Road, Henderson, Auckland

Estate bottled   11 acres of Riesling

6,000 bottles of botrytized Riesling per year

or 12,000 bottles of 'straight' Rieslings per year

Quality: 🍇🍇🍇   Price: ★★★
Best vintages: '81, '86, '89, '90

Lionel Collard is one of the great characters of the New Zealand wine scene. He has scant regard for fashion, always making his wines the way he feels best. This policy may not have won him a great many friends among his colleagues, but it has brought well-deserved critical acclaim for his fine Chardonnay, Sauvignon Blanc, and Riesling wines. He is one of the most committed Riesling wine producers in the country, having made the first varietal Riesling wine in New Zealand in 1975, and his 1981 Rhine Riesling was the nation's first dessert wine made from botrytis-affected Riesling grapes. He has lately increased his acreage of vineyards planted with Riesling, adding new plantations in Hawke's Bay and Marlborough to the existing three acres in Henderson (Auckland).

The Collard winery is now largely run by Lionel's sons Bruce and Geoff, who have both worked in the German wine-producing regions. This is reflected in the Collard Rhine Riesling wines, which are very clean and fruity, and always have some sweetness. The 'straight' Rhine Rieslings are only slightly sweet, with quite crisp acidity and full peachy fruit. The botrytized Rhine Riesling is considerably richer, but not in a full-blown raisiny style with luscious sweetness. Extremely elegant and richly fruity, it is only modestly sweet, and with delicate tropical-fruit tones from the botrytis.

GIESEN

Canterbury

Giesen Wine Estate, Burnham School Road, No. 5 R.D., Christchurch

Estate bottled   15 acres of Riesling

84,000 bottles of Riesling per year

Quality: 🍇🍇🍇   Price: ★★★ – ★★★★
Best vintages: '86, '88, '89, '90

Canterbury is the most southerly commercial wine-growing region in New Zealand, and the world (though experimental production has now begun yet further south in Wanaka). So far it has attracted the most attention with its highly touted Pinot Noir red wines. However, from my tastings the best wines from the plains of Canterbury, which stretch from the Alps of the South Island to the city of Christchurch, are the dry whites. Some of the best and most interesting have been Rieslings from the family-owned Giesen estate.

The Giesen estate was founded in 1980 at Burnham School Road, nearly twenty miles south of Christchurch, where it is run by brothers Marcel, Theo, and Alex. Their vineyards are planted on rough stony soil which, together with the region's climate of warm sunny days followed by cool nights, makes for full-bodied white wines with plenty of crisp acidity. They have some similarities to Marlborough white wines, but with less of the tropical fruit aromas that make the wines of that region so distinctive. The Giesens' Rieslings are made in a wide range of styles from full-bodied dry wines with pineappley fruit and clean lemony acidity, through lighter medium wines (the larger part of their production), to Brut sparkling wines, and lusciously honeyed dessert wines from botrytis-affected grapes.

Though the quality of the wines from the Giesens' first vintages in the mid-eighties was a little variable, the best fully realized the potential of their region. As wine-maker Marcel Giesen, who is only twenty-six years of age, gains experience some exciting wines can be expected from this estate.

MARTINBOROUGH VINEYARD

Martinborough

Martinborough Vineyard, Princess Street, P.O. Box 85, Martinborough

Estate bottled   1 acre of Riesling

2,400 bottles of Riesling per year

Quality: 🍇🍇🍇　　Price: ★★★
Best vintages: '87, '89, '90

Martinborough Vineyard is currently the only commercial producer of Riesling wines from the small Martinborough Appellation (shortly to be joined by Lintz Estate). This new wine-
producing area is at the southern tip of the North Island just
east of Wellington. The road twists its way across the Rimutaka
Range, with a precipitous drop awaiting any drivers who aren't
watching what they're doing. Martinborough (whose town plan
is in the form of a Union Jack) lies in the broad Ruamahanga
Valley between the Rimutaka and Aorangi Mountains. To these
ranges, on which cloud formations from both the east and west
deposit the rain they are carrying, it owes its exceptionally dry
climate. It is this that gives Martinborough its considerable
potential as a premium wine-producing region.

Martinborough Vineyard produced the region's first wines
in 1983. Though some of the newer arrivals on the tiny
Martinborough scene make some very good wines,
Martinborough Vineyard's Larry McKenna is probably the
most consistent wine-maker in the area. The Martinborough
Vineyard's Riesling is medium-bodied and off-dry, with full,
floral, apricoty-orangey fruit and quite crisp acidity. In some
vintages there is a touch of botrytis, giving the wine a touch of
exotic fruit character. This has encouraged Martinborough
Vineyard to plant more Riesling, so that in the future a dessert-
style wine from botrytis-affected grapes can also be made.

THE MILLTON VINEYARD

Gisborne

The Millton Vineyard, Papatu Road, Manutuke, Poverty Bay

Estate bottled　　　5 acres of Riesling

2,000 bottles of late-harvest Riesling per year

9,000 bottles of other Rieslings per year

LATE-HARVEST RIESLINGS

Quality: 🍇🍇🍇🍇   Price: ★★★

OTHER RIESLINGS

Quality: 🍇🍇🍇   Price: ★★★

Best vintages: '85, '87, '89, '90

James and Annie Millton are the only Riesling wine producers of any significance in the Gisborne area, and New Zealand's only organic wine producers. All decisions as to when they prune, trim, and spray (which they do only with copper sulphate and vegetable extracts) their vines are made according to the phases of the moon and the motions of the planets by a system called bio-dynamics. Whether one believes that bio-dynamics has some foundation or not, there is no denying the fact that Millton Vineyard make some excellent white wines.

James Millton studied wine-making in France and Germany, returning to New Zealand in 1980. He and his wife then began replanting the vineyards her father owned in Gisborne with noble vine varieties. Looked at on paper Gisborne's climatic statistics don't look ideal for Riesling wines, yet since the 1985 vintage James Millton has produced a string of rich yet elegant Rieslings. The best of these is clearly the Rhine Riesling Late Harvest (Individual Bunch Selection), a luscious highly concentrated dessert wine with intense dried apricot and marmalade aromas and flavours. In warm years this wine can be a little heavy, but the better vintages have a beautiful balance of modest alcohol, racy acidity, and honeyed sweetness. The Opou Vineyards Rhine Riesling often has a touch of botrytis character, too. Medium-bodied with a good weight of soft apricoty fruit and a touch of sweetness, it is similar to the Spätlese-style wines from the south of Germany.

NGATARAWA

Hawke's Bay

Ngatarawa Wines, Private Bag, Washpool, Hastings

Estate bottled   4 acres of Riesling

2,500 bottles of late-harvest Riesling per year

4,000 bottles of other Rieslings per year

LATE-HARVEST RIESLINGS

Quality: 🍇🍇🍇🍇   Price: ★★★★

OTHER RIESLINGS

Quality: 🍇🍇   Price: ★★

Best vintages: '87, '88, '89, '90

Alwyn Corban, a descendant of the original owners of the giant Corbans Wines group in Auckland, is one of the most talented younger wine-makers in the Hawke's Bay region. In the converted stables which serve as his winery he produces superb Cabernet Sauvignon red wines, Chardonnay, Sauvignon Blanc, and Riesling white wines. Though his red wines have earned him the most publicity his late-harvest Riesling wines are perhaps even more impressive, the best being of spectacular quality.

Hawke's Bay is a top red-wine-growing region, but not the ideal location in New Zealand for producing quality fine Riesling wines, as it is rather too warm. Like most Hawke's Bay Rieslings Alwyn Corban's 'straight' Riesling wines are off-dry and rather plump. They have plenty of peachy-sherbety fruit, but also plenty of alcohol and are a little too soft. The transformation which botrytis performs on Riesling grapes here is truly astonishing, for the dessert Riesling wines he makes from them are beautifully balanced. Although their style has recently changed in the direction of greater elegance, all have a tremendous concentration of honeyed fruit and lovely racy acidity which cuts right through their considerable sweetness.

REDWOOD VALLEY ESTATE

Nelson

Redwood Valley Estate/Weingut Seifried, P.O. Box 18, Upper Moutere, Nelson

Estate bottled   17.5 acres of Riesling

2,400 bottles of late-harvest Riesling per year

72,000 bottles of other Rieslings per year

LATE-HARVEST RIESLINGS

Quality: 🍇🍇🍇   Price: ★★★★

OTHER RIESLINGS

Quality: 🍇🍇   Price: ★★★

Best vintages: '85, '86, '89

Hermann Seifried came from Germany in the early seventies intending to work for the New Zealand Apple and Pear Marketing Board, but ended up planting a vineyard in the Nelson area of the South Island and making 'real' wines instead. During the last decade he has successfully built his property into the largest and best known in the area.

Because of his German descent it isn't perhaps surprising that Hermann Seifried is as committed to the Riesling vine variety as to Chardonnay and Sauvignon Blanc. His best wines are probably the Redwood Valley Late Rhine Riesling Beerenauslese dessert wines made from selectively harvested botrytis-affected grapes. They are big, rich wines, with a bouquet of dried apricots and raisins, mouth-filling honeyed richness, and enough acidity to leave the mouth clean. The Rhine Riesling Late-Vintage wines are also honeyed, but less sweet, with the best vintages having a lovely racy acidity. Hermann Seifried's Rhine Riesling Dry and 'straight' Rhine Riesling (in a medium-sweet style) are competently made wines, but a little broad with rather plain flavours. They are best drunk young while youthful freshness gives them most appeal.

RONGOPAI

Te Kauwhata

Rongopai Wines, 71 Waerenga Road, Te Kauwhata

Estate bottled   1.5 acres of Riesling

4,000 bottles of Riesling per year

Quality: 🍇🍇🍇   Price: ★★★★

Best vintages: '85, '86, '89

Rongopai Wines made their reputation with their debut vintage, 1985, which consisted only of rich dessert wines made from selected botrytis-affected Riesling, Sauvignon Blanc, and Müller-Thurgau grapes. The winery is run by German-born and trained Dr Rainer Eschenbruch and Tom Van Dam, who both worked for the government viticultural research station in Te Kauwhata until Rongopai was launched. In 1981, while directing the wine-making research programme at Te Kauwhata, Rainer Eschenbruch became fascinated by the potential for producing dessert wines from late-harvested and botrytis-affected grapes. Shortly afterwards he went into partnership with Tom Van Dam and founded Rongopai Wines.

The Rongopai Riesling wines are always extremely clean and very well balanced, with honeyed sweetness from botrytis. However, the examples which I tasted in New Zealand did not impress me as much as they have the domestic wine press.

USA

Total vineyard area: 850,000 acres

Vineyard area planted with Riesling: 1.5%/12,000 acres

Average annual Riesling production: 60,000,000 bottles

Although most famous for its Chardonnay white wines and Cabernet Sauvignon red wines, the USA produces some of the best Riesling wines outside the classic European regions. However, the majority of the Riesling wines produced in the USA are rather simple, slightly sweet commercial wines lacking much Riesling character. It is only in the hands of a small elite group of wine-makers in New York State on the East Coast, and in California and Washington States on the West Coast, that the variety gives wines which are rich and intensely fruity, yet crisp and elegant.

Riesling arrived in the USA with European immigrants in the middle of the last century, and was first planted here by the Hungarian Agoston Haraszthy at his Buena Vista winery in Sonoma County, California, in 1857, and by the German Frank Stock in San Jose, California, at about the same time. They were rapidly followed by George Crane in 1859 at St Helena, Napa County, California, and by Charles Lefranc in 1862 in Santa Clara County, California. What enabled the variety to establish itself in California successfully, along with the wine industry as a whole, was the economic boom which the 1849 Gold Rush brought to the state. The first Riesling vines were planted in Washington State a little later in 1871 by the German Herke family at Tampico in the Yakima Valley.

Riesling's arrival in the other states of the Union came much later, in most cases during the early 1960s, when, as a result of the high reputation of German Riesling wines in the US market, American vintners attempted to imitate this style of wine. During the seventies Riesling established itself as an important grape variety for fine-wine production in California, Oregon, Washington, Idaho, New York, and Virginia. Plantings were made in numerous other states too, but on a very small scale. Quite drinkable Riesling wines are now produced in such places as Michigan (Château Grand Traverse).

Nowhere in the world did the reputation of Riesling wines suffer more during the late seventies and early eighties than in the USA. Here the Riesling revival has so far made only slow and modest progress in the face of Chardonnay's dominant position as *the* white grape variety which most American wine drinkers are aware of. It would be all too easy for a European writer mistakenly to attribute this lack of recognition of Riesling wines' greatness in the USA to a general lack of wine culture. In fact, it is due to no more than a lack of awareness. Riesling wines of domestic and foreign origin simply aren't promoted strongly enough in the USA market to make a big impact.

California

Total vineyard area: 324,000 acres

Area planted with Riesling: 2.5%/8,000 acres

Average annual Riesling production: 35,000,000 bottles

Officially, wine production in California dates from the planting of a vineyard at the Spanish mission in San Diego in 1769. Noble grape varieties, which in all likelihood included Riesling, were first brought to California by Count Agoston Haraszthy, who founded Buena Vista winery in the Carneros region immediately north of San Francisco Bay in 1857. But the real history of California's wine industry begins with the lifting of prohibition in 1934, and the move to fine-wine production

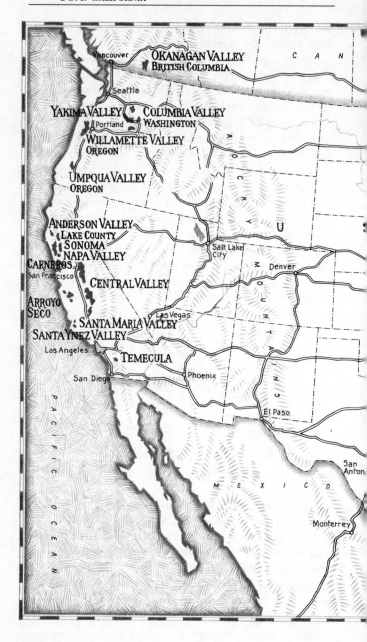

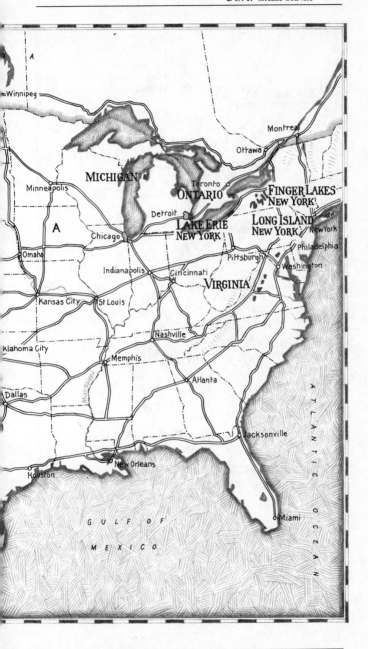

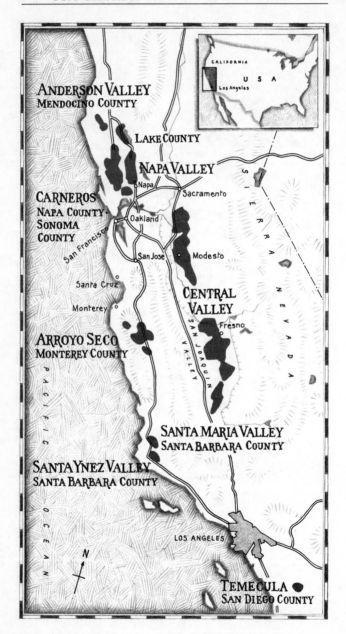

didn't begin until the sixties. During the last few years the growth has been staggering.

With only 2.5 per cent of the vineyard area, Riesling would look to be a rather minor speciality in the state. However, this relatively small acreage is widely scattered from the northern extremity of the state's vineyards round Ukiah in Mendocino County, down to Temecula, close to San Diego in the far south. Riesling wines tend to be produced by Californian wineries in small quantities for sale to visitors. As a result there are over 300 producers of Riesling wines in California – a paradoxical position given the small acreage.

The reason for this popularity is the change in style of Riesling wines which took place in California nearly twenty years ago. Until then Riesling grapes were harvested early, and the wine fermented dry. It was refreshingly crisp, but not very fruity or characterful. Around 1970 a number of producers started deliberately harvesting Riesling later and making the wines with a touch of sweetness. Though these wines were often a bit too soft, they had a full apricot/citrus fruit character which made them easy drinking.

At about the same time Californian wine producers discovered how botrytis could be used to make Riesling dessert wines. Kurt Wente of Livermore is credited with the discovery of botrytis in California during the 1969 harvest at his vineyards in Arroyo Seco, Monterey County. He made small amounts of late-harvest Rieslings from botrytized grapes in '72 and '73, and the word spread. A group of specialists quickly made a name for themselves as producers of super-luscious Riesling dessert wines, which were internationally acclaimed as being of world class.

The Californian Riesling 'boom' came to its peak at the beginning of the eighties, with the vineyard area in production rising to over 10,000 acres in 1984. However, the fashion for drier French-style white wines, and particularly for the Chardonnay variety, was already beginning to make itself felt by this time. Now only a few specialists continue to make Riesling wines from conviction. Thankfully, their wines are extremely impressive.

Though it is difficult to find fine dry or off-dry Riesling wines in California, there are a number of producers of spectacular dessert wines. They are often very rich and honeyed, with a strong dried fruits or raisiny character which gives them great power. They can easily accompany all but the sweetest and richest of desserts. Though they lack the finesse of a German Riesling Beerenauslesen or Trockenbeerenauslesen, or the muscular elegance of an Alsace Vendange Tardive, it's easy to be seduced by their sheer lusciousness. Beware, though: in a few cases it's difficult to believe that the wines are really from Riesling grapes, since instead of the elegant interplay of fruit and acidity so typical of fine Riesling wines, you get liquid Disneyland!

THE PROPOSED CLASSIFICATION

The Wine Institute of California has put forward a classification for late-harvested Riesling wines similar to the German Prädikat system. Unless noted otherwise, it is used by the producers described in this guide. It is to be hoped that others will follow suit, since it is better that tongue-twister terms such as 'Individual Dried Bunch Select Late Harvest' be abandoned – however sad the loss of the abbreviation IDBSLH is.

Late Harvest	(Auslese)	Minimum 102.5° Öchsle
Select Late Harvest	(Beerenauslese)	Minimum 120° Öchsle
Special Select Late Harvest	(Trocken-beerenauslese)	Minimum 152.5° Öchsle

CHÂTEAU ST JEAN

Sonoma County

Château St Jean, 8555 Sonoma Highway, Kenwood, CA 95452

3,000 bottles of late-harvest Riesling per year

120,000 bottles of Riesling per year

LATE-HARVEST RIESLING

Quality: 🍇🍇🍇🍇🍇   Price: ★★★★★

OTHER RIESLINGS

Quality: 🍇🍇   Price: ★★★

Best vintages: '77, '78, '80, '81, '82, '83, '85, '86, '88, '90

Château St Jean was founded in 1973 and with their first wine, a 1974 Selected Late-Harvest Johannisberg Riesling, wine-maker Richard Arrowwood established a reputation for the winery as one of the top producers in Sonoma County. The Château's reputation slumped somewhat at the beginning of the eighties, but since the Japanese liquor corporation Suntory bought the winery in 1984 it has rapidly rebuilt its good name.

St Jean's late-harvested Johannisberg Riesling wines are all vineyard designated, usually coming from Robert Young Vineyards or Belle Terre Vineyards, both in Sonoma County's Alexander Valley, with whom St Jean has long-term contracts. The pickers here make several passes through the Riesling vineyards, each harvest selecting botrytized grapes. Here botrytized Riesling grapes can be harvested every vintage, and Richard Arrowwood has been able to gather a lot of experience in making these wines within a very short period of time.

Richard Arrowwood's greatest successes are his extremely luscious dessert wines, overflowing with apricot, citrus, and honey aromas. In spite of their enormous concentration of flavour and high sweetness, they are never heavy or fat, but always clean and well balanced. Since the 1981 vintage the Château has used the Wine Institute's classification system for late-harvested wines (p. 184), though here the level of richness is often way above the required minimums. Until the 1980 vintage St Jean's classification for late-harvested Johannisberg Riesling wines ran, in ascending order of richness, Late Harvest (Spätlese equivalent), Selected Late Harvest (Auslese), Individual Bunch Selected Late Harvest (Beerenauslese), individual Dried Bunch Select Late Harvest (Trockenbeerenauslese).

The Sonoma County Riesling from St Jean is a pleasant, well-made wine, but lacks the complexity which the strong botrytis character gives the late-harvest wines. It is best drunk shortly after release, when its soft peachy fruit is most pronounced.

FIRESTONE VINEYARD

Santa Ynez Valley, Santa Barbara County

Firestone Vineyard, P.O. Box 244, Los Olivos, CA 93441

240,000 bottles of Riesling per year

3,600 bottles of late-harvest Riesling each suitable vintage

LATE-HARVEST RIESLING

Quality: 🍇🍇🍇   Price: ★★★★

OTHER RIESLINGS

Quality: 🍇🍇   Price: ★★

Best vintages: '82, '85, '88

Brooks Firestone, son of Harvey Firestone, founder of the Firestone Tyre & Rubber Company, describes himself as 'an executive dropout'. Together with wine-maker Alison Green he produces some of the best wines in the Santa Ynez Valley at his Suntory-backed winery. Of the Californian Riesling wines produced in large volumes Firestone's 'straight' Johannisberg Riesling must be the best. It is quite crisp, with modest sweetness, and has attractive peachy fruit with a hint of coconut in the bouquet. Night picking and the coolish climate of the Santa Ynez Valley account for the wine's elegance.

The Ambassador's Vineyard Select Late-Harvest Johannisberg Rieslings are more complex. They are somewhat reminiscent of lighter German Beerenauslese wines, with a delicately honeyed botrytis aroma, sweet, richly honeyed palate, and just enough acidity to balance. Unusually for California, they are matured for a short period in small French oak casks, though no smell or taste of oak can be detected in the finished wines. They drink well from release and are at their best within five or six years of the harvest.

FREEMARK ABBEY

Napa Valley

Freemark Abbey, 3022 St Helena Highway N, St Helena, CA 94574

1,800 bottles of late-harvest Riesling per year

26,000 bottles of Riesling per year

LATE-HARVEST RIESLING

Quality: 🍇🍇🍇🍇   Price: ★★★★★

OTHER RIESLINGS

Quality: 🍇🍇🍇   Price: ★★★

Best vintages: '73, '76, '78, '82, '86, '88, '90

Freemark Abbey was the first Californian winery to market a late-harvested Riesling made from botrytis-affected grapes. This was their 1973 Edelwein, made by then wine-maker Jerry Luper, and it caused a sensation. The wine was superb when young, and though fully mature this landmark wine was still deliciously honeyed when tasted in 1986. With the 1976 vintage Freemark Abbey introduced a higher grade of Riesling dessert wine, Edelwein Gold, and they have stuck with these unique designations to the present day.

The Freemark Abbey Edelwein and Edelwein Gold are

rather more restrained than the majority of Californian late-harvested Riesling wines. They have a pronounced lemony acidity and quite subtle botrytis character, showing more exotic fruit flavours than the dried fruits and raisininess typical of such wines. In their youth, they can seem a little too sweet, but after a couple of years in bottle they have good balance. The winery's 'straight' Johannisberg Rieslings also have quite a pronounced acidity, which makes them taste considerably lighter than their 12° or so of alcohol would suggest. They often need a couple of years in the bottle to soften. Fermented off-dry, they have excellent length of flavour for Californian Rieslings, and are good food wines.

HIDDEN CELLARS

Mendocino County

Hidden Cellars, 1500 Ruddick-Cunningham Road, Ukiah, CA 95482

24,000 bottles of Riesling per year

2,000 bottles of late-harvest Riesling each suitable vintage

LATE-HARVEST RIESLING

Quality: 🍇🍇🍇🍇   Price: ★★★★

OTHER RIESLINGS

Quality: 🍇🍇   Price: ★★

Best vintages: '85, '86, '88, '90

Far away from fashionable Napa and Sonoma Valleys, at Ukiah, at the northern end of Mendocino County, Dennis Patton makes a wide range of well-crafted elegant white and red wines. What started as a hobby winery has now become one of the most important commercial operations in the county. Along with fellow Mendocino producers Navarro, Hidden Cellars is one of the few Californian wineries to receive widespread press acclaim for its Rieslings. This is well justified, for the wines are among the best Rieslings in the state.

Hidden Cellars' 'straight' Johannisberg Rieslings come from
Potter Valley in Mendocino. They have about 11.5° of alcohol,
are soft, grapey and flowery, with a hint of marzipan on the
palate and nice citrusy acidity. Attractive as they are, a touch
less sweetness would allow the abundant fruit to show a little
more strongly. It is in the late-harvest category that Hidden
Cellars has so far made its best Riesling wines. Extremely rich
and sweet, yet not overwhelming, they are packed with spicy
botrytis and dried apricot flavours.

JEKEL

Arroyo Seco, Monterey County

Jekel, 40155 Walnut Av., Greenfield, CA 93927

70 acres of Riesling

200,000 bottles of Riesling per year

9,000 bottles of late-harvest Riesling per year

LATE-HARVEST RIESLING

Quality: 🍇🍇🍇🍇   Price: ★★★

OTHER RIESLINGS

Quality: 🍇🍇   Price: ★★

Best vintages: '78, '79, '80, '81, '82, '85, '86, '88, '90

Before Bill Jekel became a wine producer he studied law, ran
companies building scenery and backdrops for film and television, and made television commercials. Perhaps for this
reason he has a most unconventional, even iconoclastic,
approach to some of the wine industry's holy cows. Bill Jekel's
loudly and oft-repeated contention that the vineyard soil has no
influence on the resulting wine's character has attracted angry
responses.

The Jekel Riesling wines caused quite a stir when they first
came onto the market at the end of the seventies. They have a
lean, appley acidity, some carbon dioxide, which gives them a

prickle on the tongue, and are quite full-bodied and flowery. Jekel produce four different grades of Riesling: dry; 'regular', which is lightly sweet; sweet, which is really quite sweet; and late-harvest, which is lusciously sweet. The higher up the scale one goes the more botrytis-affected grapes went into the press, and the more interesting the wines become, taking on extra layers of fruit and honeyed flavours and aromas.

Under new wine-maker Steve Pessagno the Jekel late-harvest Rieslings are being made in a more elegant style (as of the '88 vintage), and can now be compared with all but the very best wines in this style made in Germany.

NAVARRO VINEYARDS

Anderson Valley, Mendocino County

Navarro Vineyards, Box 47, Philo, CA 95466

Estate bottled   10 acres of Riesling

8,000 bottles of Riesling per year

8,000 bottles of late-harvest Riesling per year

Quality: 𝅏𝅏𝅏𝅏𝅏   Price: ★★★ – ★★★★★

Best vintages: '83, '85, '86, '87, '88, '90

Ted Bennet sold his Pacific Stereo chain of electrical stores to CBS in 1974 and moved to remote Anderson Valley with his wife Barbara Cahn to found Navarro Vineyards. The cool, foggy climate of Anderson Valley is ideal for Riesling, and has enabled Ted Bennet to produce a string of Riesling wines with an elegance unsurpassed for California. As Ted himself puts it, 'due to our miserable climate we can make very fine Rieslings', which also gives a good idea of how modest and affable Ted Bennet is. However, such remarkably high-quality wines aren't easily produced even with the climatic 'advantages' of Anderson Valley. Early vintages from Navarro were sometimes very rough and ready, but with hand-picking at night, cool fermentation in stainless steel, and maturation in large casks of old German oak Ted Bennet has found a winning wine-making formula.

The straight Navarro White Riesling is already a wine of the highest quality, combining the body of a fine Alsace Riesling with the filigree fruitiness of a Riesling wine from Germany's Rheingau region. Usually it has around 12° of alcohol, but the firm acidity and a touch of sweetness harmonize this beautifully. The peachy flavours at the front, racy acidity, and long finish make it a stand-out wine of an elegance ideally suited to the dining table.

The late-harvest Cluster Selected wine is a rich botrytized Riesling dessert wine of astonishing elegance and finesse. It generally has about 10° of alcohol, and its high natural acidity gives it a scintillating brilliance on the palate unlike anything else to be found in the state. The apricot and dried peach flavours are extremely rich, yet also finely etched. The often high residual sweetness never dominates or obtrudes. Tasting recent vintages (off the chopping block in Ted's kitchen) it is hard to believe that Ted Bennet threw away the botrytized grapes from his Riesling harvests until 1979! 'I console myself with the fact that it took man 3,000 years to discover how to make sweet wines from botrytized grapes, and it only took me five years,' he told me.

NEWLAN

Napa Valley

Newlan, 5225 St Helena Highway, Napa, CA 94558

Estate bottled

2,400 bottles of late-harvest Riesling each suitable vintage

Quality: 🍇🍇🍇🍇   Price: ★★★★

Best vintages: '78, '82, '86, '88, '90

Bruce Newlan founded his winery, which was originally known as Alatera Vineyards, in 1977. Renamed Newlan in 1981, it is a family-run enterprise in the fullest sense, something rather rare in big-business-dominated Napa Valley.

The Newlans' Riesling vineyard is situated directly next to the Napa river at the cooler southern end of the valley. Here it only takes a little moisture in September to give fully botrytized Riesling grapes by mid-October. Bruce Newlan noticed this immediately, and made his first Late-Harvest Bunch Selected Johannisberg Riesling in 1978. He has learnt quickly and his 1982 won the Lingenfelder trophy for botrytis wines at the International Wine and Spirit competition in London in September 1988. However, recent vintages are even better, the wines showing remarkable delicacy for Napa Valley late-harvest Rieslings. The concentrated peachy-lemony fruit is off-set by mouth-watering acidity, which beautifully balances the very high sweetness.

JOSEPH PHELPS

Spring Valley (Napa Valley)

Joseph Phelps, 200 Taplin Road, P.O. Box 1031, St Helena, CA 94574

Estate bottled   32 acres of Riesling

75,000 bottles of Riesling per year

15,000 bottles of late-harvest Riesling per year

LATE-HARVEST RIESLING

Quality: 🍇🍇🍇🍇   Price: ★★★★ – ★★★★★

OTHER RIESLING

Quality: 🍇🍇🍇   Price: ★★★

Best vintages: '75, '77, '78, '79, '80, '81, '82, '83, '86, '88, '90

Like Château St Jean in Sonoma County, Joseph Phelps made their name with their first release, a 1973 Johannisberg Riesling. Also like Château St Jean, Phelps stuck with Riesling in spite of its reduced popularity in the USA during the early eighties.

Joe Phelps's winery is one of the few in the valley not to make an aggressive architectural statement, its long, low timber construction hugging a hillside high above the plain of Napa Valley. Here, in marked contrast to the trend in California towards one-variety wineries, Phelps make a remarkably wide variety of wines.

Wine-maker Craig Williams continues to make the style of Riesling which Phelps's first wine-maker, German Walter Schug, introduced. The Phelps Rieslings, whether early harvested off-dry wines or rich late-harvest wines, are always very clean. Sometimes a little lean when released, all these styles can mature for a decade and more. The early harvested wines are crisp and floral, while the top (select) late-harvest Rieslings have complex buttery, peachy, apricot, and raisiny flavours. However, I'm not convinced that the dessert Riesling wines being made at Phelps today are quite as good as those of the seventies and early eighties.

TREFETHEN

Napa Valley

Trefethen, 1160 Oak Knoll Ave., P.O. Box 2460, Napa, CA 94558

Estate bottled   32 acres of Riesling

66,000 bottles of white Riesling per year

Quality: 🍇🍇🍇   Price: ★★★

Best vintages: '85, '86, '88, '90

The Trefethen winery, previously known as the Eshcol estate, is one of the oldest and most beautiful winery buildings in the Napa Valley. It was built in 1886, and up until the end of the last century it was one of the leading wineries among

Napa Valley's 143 wine producers. When Katie and Gene Trefethen bought the old Eshcol estate in 1968 the Napa Valley
renaissance was only just beginning. They replanted the
600 acres of vineyards and made the first Trefethen wines in
1973.

Though Trefethen's Riesling vineyards are situated in the
cooler southerly part of Napa Valley the grapes none the less
ripen far enough for the wines to have 12° of natural alcohol.
They are fermented almost to dryness, are crisp, and have most
attractive ripe apple and peach flavours. In the best vintages the
finish is long, and the wines have a remarkable delicacy considering their alcoholic content.

MARK WEST VINEYARDS & WINERY

Russian River Valley, Sonoma County

Mark West Vineyards & Winery, 7000 Trenton-Healdsburg
Road, Forestville, CA 95436

Estate bottled   10 acres of Riesling

20,000 bottles of Riesling per year

4,800 bottles of late-harvest Riesling each suitable vintage

Quality: 🍇🍇🍇   Price: ★★ – ★★★★★

Best vintages: '83, '86

What is it that gives airline pilots a compulsion to become
wine-makers in Sonoma County's coolest grape-growing
region, Russian River Valley? Both Bob Ellis, who founded
Mark West in 1976, and Joseph Swan, the area's Pinot Noir
guru, were airline pilots before they turned to wine-making.
Perhaps the dense fog which hangs in the valley well into the
morning most days reminded them of the clouds.

Russian River Valley has become known within California
during the last few years as perhaps the most suitable area of the
whole state for Pinot Noir. On the basis of Mark West's Ries-

lings it might also be the most promising area for Riesling. Fermented almost to bone-dryness, Riesling wines contain around 12° of alcohol but have surprisingly delicate white peach and almond flavours, and elegant appley-lemony acidity. They are typical examples of Bob Ellis's 'understated, elegant' style of wine-making. Unlike most Californian Rieslings they make excellent 'food wines'.

New York State

Total vineyard area: 46,500 acres

Vineyard area planted with Riesling: less than 1%

Wine has been produced in New York State for more than three centuries, and Brotherhood Valley Winery in Washingtonville in the Hudson valley, founded in 1839, is the oldest winery in North America. Outside North America its wines are little known, and until recently this may have been no bad thing, for only recently have interesting wines from noble grape varieties been produced here. The great majority of New York State's wine production is still wines made from native vine varieties (which are all types of *Vitis labrusca*), and hybrids between these and classic French vine varieties. The former give wines with a 'foxy' smell and taste, the latter yield adequate but rather characterless wines. More than half New York's grape production is used for grape juice and marmalade, and fully 25 per cent of the wine production is 'New York State Champagne' (made largely from hybrid grapes).

With only forty years' history in the region the noble *Vitis vinifera* varieties still account for only a tiny portion of the state's production. Of them Riesling is one of the more important, but perhaps as much by reason of its sheer hardiness as because of the New York wine growers' love of the variety's wines. If Riesling has difficulty in the majority of California's wine-growing regions because they are too warm, in New York State it is much more at home. Here its grapes struggle somewhat to ripen just as they often do in the more northerly wine-growing regions of Germany. If many of the resulting wines are rather boring, a few wineries have shown that in the right place the Riesling vine can produce first-class wines in New York.

Of the four wine-growing regions in the state, Finger Lakes, just south of Lake Ontario, shows the greatest potential. Here the harsh continental climate is considerably moderated by the influence of the deep Finger Lakes (which were carved out by glaciers during the ice age) and of Lake Ontario. Particularly around Dundee on the western shore of Seneca Lake some elegant Riesling wines rather reminiscent of those from the Mosel valley in Germany are produced. It was in this area that *Vitis vinifera* vines were pioneered in New York by Dr Konstantin Frank during the fifties.

The largest of New York State's wine-growing regions, Lake Erie, also shows some potential for Riesling, though premium-quality wine production here is much less advanced than around Finger Lakes. In spite of having more than 20,000 acres under vines there are only seven wineries here, compared to the forty-two in Finger Lakes area.

The youngest of the state's wine-growing regions, Long Island, also shows some promise, but the mild maritime climate here is perhaps too warm for Riesling.

HERON HILL

Finger Lakes

Heron Hill Vineyards, Hammondsport, New York 14840

Estate bottled   25 acres of Riesling

20,000 bottles of Riesling per year

Quality: 🍇🍇🍇   Price: ★★★
Best vintages: '86, '88, '90

Heron Hill Vineyards on the western bank of Keuka Lake has a
dramatic history which says much about the development of
wine-growing in New York State. The twenty-five-acre home
vineyard was first planted in 1968, but just as the native Con-
cord and Catawba vines were starting to bear fruit the entire
vineyard was grubbed up and replanted with Riesling and
Chardonnay vines. The consistently fine quality achieved with
these varieties has made Heron Hill one of the most renowned
wineries of the entire Finger Lakes region.

The winery produces Riesling wines under two labels. The
Heron Hill wines are medium-bodied and off-dry with a pronounced acidity that makes them taste very dry, and they are
definitely food wines (seafood!). The finer-quality Riesling
wines (made only from the free-run juice) are sold under the
Otter Spring label. They are more filigrain, their bracing
acidity balanced by an obvious touch of sweetness. Several
impressive late-harvested dessert wines have also been produced and sold under the Otter Spring label.

HERMANN J. WIEMER

Finger Lakes

Hermann J. Wiemer Vineyard, Route 14, Dundee, New
   York 14837

Estate bottled   40 acres of Riesling

98,000 bottles of Riesling per year

Quality: 🍇🍇🍇🍇   Price: ★★★ – ★★★★
Best vintages: '84, '86, '88, '90

Hermann J. Wiemer makes the finest Riesling wines in New
York State from his vineyards on the western shore of Seneca
Lake in the Finger Lakes region. Hermann Wiemer was born

in Bernkastel on the Mosel in Germany, and after completing his education as wine-maker he moved to New York and became wine-maker at Bully Hill Vineyards. He planted ninety acres of his own vineyards in 1973, and launched his first wine (a '79 Johannisberg Riesling) in 1980 shortly after leaving Bully Hill. Within a few years he was widely acclaimed as one of the state's star wine-makers.

His Riesling wines are extremely elegant, with crisp, sharply defined appley and peachy fruit, and taste much lighter than they actually are (around 11.5° of alcohol). They are more than a little reminiscent of the Riesling wines of Hermann Wiemer's home town in Germany. The Dry Johannisberg Riesling is bone-dry, but not at all lean or hard. The 'straight' Johannisberg Riesling is just off-dry, and has an excellent balance of fruit, acidity, and alcohol. Hermann Wiemer's star wine is his Bunch Select Late Harvest, which is undoubtedly the finest Riesling wine produced east of the Rocky Mountains. In contrast to the massive raisiny richness of most late-harvested Riesling wines from California, it is sleek and refined, with a scintillating interplay of concentrated dried peach fruit and racy acidity. He also produces a small quantity of Riesling sparkling wines.

WOODBURY

Lake Erie

Woodbury Vineyards, South Roberts Road, Dunkirk, New York 14048

Estate bottled   40 acres of Riesling

24,000 bottles of Riesling per year

Quality: 🍇🍇🍇   Price: ★★★

Best vintages: '80, '84, '88

Brothers Bob and Gary Woodbury run the most dynamic winery on the southern shore of Lake Erie in upstate New

York. They began as grape growers, planting their first vineyards in 1970 after taking over the family farm in 1967. Unusually for the region, they started with noble *Vitis vinifera* varieties, convinced that the climate on Lake Erie wasn't too cold to ripen Riesling and Chardonnay grapes. In fact on the southern shore of Lake Erie the growing season is significantly longer than in Finger Lakes. After seeing that the quality of the grapes coming from their vineyards was good they decided to take the plunge and become wine-makers in 1979.

The result is crisply fruity, aromatic Riesling wines lighter than anything else produced in North America. In lesser vintages they can be just a little green and tart, but the best are long and elegant in flavour, with very appealing coconut and white peach flavours. The 'straight' Riesling is medium-dry, the Dry Riesling a steely bone-dry wine. Since 1981 the Woodburys have also produced a Riesling sparkling wine. It is crisp and appley, with subtle bready-yeast flavours giving some complexity.

Oregon

Total vineyard area: 4,900 acres

Vineyard area planted with Riesling: 18%/890 acres

Average annual Riesling production: 2,400,000 bottles

Oregon's history as a producer of wines from the noble European grape varieties is no longer than that of Washington State immediately to its north, a mere quarter century. However, in that short time the state's wineries have been remarkably successful in gaining recognition for themselves beyond the north-western states. This has largely been the result of the elegant, fruity Pinot Noir red wines which they have been making since the early eighties. With the Californian market next door thirsty for high-class Chardonnay white wines, it isn't perhaps surprising that this is the white variety which has gained Oregon wine-growers the most attention. While the majority of the state's wineries also produce Riesling wines, these have hitherto received little attention and tend to be regarded by their producers as little more than 'cash-flow' wines for quick sale (often through winery tasting rooms, as in California).

The reasons for this are, I believe, fundamentally climatic. Most of Oregon's vineyards lie in the Willamette Valley just to the west and south of Portland, about forty miles from the Pacific coast. The climate here is warmer than in the main vineyard regions of Washington State, and also much wetter. Riesling wines are not an important part of any winery's range here, and in comparison to the care taken to find the best possible sites for Pinot Noir vineyards, Riesling has tended to be planted wherever is convenient. As a result, the Riesling wines produced in Oregon are a very mixed bag. At their rare best they can match the finest from the Yakima Valley in Washington. These are usually medium-bodied off-dry wines of which the best have been those from Elk Cove, though a few fine dessert wines have recently been produced (e.g. by Henry Winery). However, a great many Oregon Rieslings are rather alcoholic and fruitless.

Washington State

Total vineyard area: 10,200 acres

Vineyard area planted with Riesling: 26%/2,650 acres

Average annual Riesling production: 16,000,000 bottles

Of all the wine-producing regions of North America, Washington State's vineyards have the greatest potential for fine-quality Riesling wines. Situated 200 miles east of the coastline in the Columbia and Yakima Valleys, and at Walla Walla, they enjoy a very different climate from rainswept Seattle and Tacoma further west. The Columbia and Yakima Valleys are virtual deserts, with less than 10 inches of rain per year. The summers are warm, though temperatures rarely go far above 90°F, and the long sunny days are followed by cool nights. The winters can be bitterly cold. Irrigation of the sandy volcanic soils is essential here for vines to grow, but apart from this conditions are very favourable for producing high-quality white wines.

Riesling has been grown in Washington State since 1871, but commercial production began only in the 1960s. The state's reputation for Riesling wines dates from the 1972 vintage Riesling produced by its largest winery, Château Ste Michelle. During the late seventies there was a dramatic expansion of the state's vineyard area, plantations of Riesling increasing from 519 acres in 1978 to 2,380 acres in 1982! Washington's reputation as a quality wine-producing region has been largely built upon its Rieslings, though its Chardonnay and Sauvignon Blanc white wines and its Merlot and Cabernet Sauvignon red wines are also attracting attention now.

Given the emphasis placed on Riesling in Washington State, the general quality of its Riesling wines is a little disappointing, though the best have complex finely nuanced peach, pear, and subtle exotic fruit, and an elegant balance of fruit, alcohol, and ripe acidity. A handful of producers are regularly making fine-quality wines in a range of styles from bone-dry, through lighter off-dry and medium-dry wines, to rich dessert wines from grapes affected by botrytis.

CHÂTEAU STE MICHELLE

Château Ste Michelle, 1 Stimson Lane, Woodinville, WA 98072

672 acres of Riesling

4,000,000 bottles of Riesling per year

LATE-HARVEST RIESLING (CHÂTEAU RESERVE)

Quality: 🍇🍇🍇🍇   Price: ★★★★

OTHER RIESLINGS

Quality: 👑   Price: ★★ – ★★★

Best vintages: '84, '85, '88, '89

Stimson Lane is the giant of Washington State, owning Château Ste Michelle, the state's largest winery, and Columbia Crest, the second largest. They produced the first wine in Washington State from a noble *Vitis vinifera* variety in 1967, and they are the largest producer of Riesling wines in the state. As its name suggests, Château Ste Michelle is based in a château-style building just outside Seattle, which houses the offices of Stimson Lane. It has two further facilities – at Grand-view in the Yakima Valley, where the majority of the wines sold under the Château Ste Michelle label are made, and the Col-umbia Crest winery at Paterson in the Columbia Valley.

It isn't perhaps surprising that the wines produced by such a huge company with such extensive vineyards should vary con-siderably in quality. Both Ste Michelle's and Columbia Crest's 'straight' Riesling wines are made in a medium-dry style, the latter slightly sweeter than the former. The Ste Michelle Col-umbia Valley Johannisberg Riesling is clearly the better, with quite forthright peachy–apricoty fruit and a crisp slightly citrusy finish. The Columbia Crest Johannisberg Riesling is more obvious, seeming much sweeter and less elegant. The Château Ste Michelle White Riesling from Columbia Valley also seems quite sweet, with rich apricoty fruit, but is recom-mended only to those looking for a distinctly sweet wine.

In quite a different class altogether are the late-harvested Riesling wines sold under the Château Reserve label of Château Ste Michelle. They are among the most impressive Riesling wines produced in the state, and are certainly the richest. The super-ripe fruit aromas and flavours which the intensely sunny summers of the Yakima Valley can give the Riesling grapes here, and the tart crispness from the region's cool nights, seem distilled in a wine that comes close to matching the complexity of the finest European dessert Rieslings.

COLUMBIA CREST

See Château Ste Michelle

THE HOGUE CELLARS

> The Hogue Cellars, Wine Country Road, P.O. Box 31, Prosser WA 99350
>
> 40,000 bottles of Riesling per year
>
> Quality: 🍇🍇🍇🍇   Price: ★★★
>
> Best vintages: '88, '89

Mike and Gary Hogue own 1,200 acres of farmland scattered in a three-mile radius round Prosser in the Yakima Valley. Mike Hogue founded the Hogue Cellars in 1982 and has rapidly built the family company into the third largest winery in the state. Under wine-maker Rob Griffin, who joined Hogue in 1984, they have also become the state's most consistent producer of fine-quality Riesling wines. In numerous competitions Hogue Rieslings have won medals and accolades.

The Hogues have 220 acres of vineyards, from which they make a wide range of red and white varietal wines. Four different Riesling wines are produced each year, of which two are dry. The finer of these, the Schwartzman Vineyard Dry Johannisberg Riesling, is perhaps the best dry Riesling wine produced in North America, coming quite close in style to the best dry Riesling wines from the more southerly regions of Germany. It is medium-bodied with intense peachy fruit and complex spicy–earthy overtones in the bouquet and on the palate. The 'straight' Yakima Valley Dry Riesling is almost as good, lacking a little of the complexity of the Schwartzman Vineyard wine, but making up for this with its forthright peach and pear fruitiness. It is delightful from release, while the Schwartzman Vineyard wine benefits from at least a year in bottle.

Two Rieslings with varying degrees of sweetness are also made by Rob Griffin. The Yakima Valley Johannisberg

Riesling is the simplest wine in the Hogue Riesling range, but still delightful. It has similarly attractive aromas and flavours to the dry Yakima Valley wine, but with a medium-dry balance. The Markin Vineyard Late-Harvest White Riesling is the top of the range. It has very intense fruit, is quite sweet, and has the highest acidity of the Hogue Rieslings. This wine must be experienced to be believed. No other Riesling I've tasted outside Europe has anything like its pure seductive peachiness.

KIONA VINEYARDS

Kiona Vineyards and Winery, RT2, Box 219E, Benton City, WA 99320

5 acres of Riesling

15,000 bottles of late-harvest Riesling per year

45,000 bottles of other Rieslings per year

Quality: 🍇🍇🍇   Price: ★★★ – ★★★★

Best vintages: '85, '86, '88, '89, '90

Kiona Vineyards is one of the smallest wineries in Washington State, producing less than 150,000 bottles of wine per year. Like most wineries in the state, Kiona make a range of varietal wines. All their white wines have very forthright fruit character, and the aromas virtually leap out of the glass at you. Perhaps some will find them a little unsubtle, but hedonists who love wines bursting with fruit will love Kiona's white wines.

Their Riesling wines show lush peachy and apricoty aromas and flavours and softish acidity, and are full-bodied wines compared to the majority of Rieslings produced in Washington. The 'straight' Johannisberg Riesling has a fruit-salad bouquet and juicy off-dry palate of no great sophistication. Much more impressive is the White Riesling Late Harvest, which has an impressive creamy richness, with subtle honeyed aromas from botrytis. This is a big mouthful of wine, but in spite of its 12° of alcohol and highish sweetness it is by no means heavy.

Because winter arrives in the Yakima Valley as early as

October, ice wines made from grapes harvested while naturally frozen in the vineyard can be made. Kiona's White Riesling Ice Wines are luscious dessert wines. Their intense honeyed apricot and passion fruit bouquet is very seductive, showing classic ice-wine character, but on the palate they lack some of the steely backbone which makes German ice wines so exciting.

STEWART VINEYARDS

Stewart Vineyards, 1381 W. Riverside Avenue, Sunnyside, WA 98944

24,000 bottles of Riesling per year

Quality: 🍇🍇🍇   Price: ★★★

Best vintages: '84, '85, '88, '89

Stewart Vineyards was founded by Dr George Stewart in 1974. The grapes he grew were sold to other wineries until 1983, when he established his own winery on Cherry Hill, overlooking the Yakima Valley. From the beginning Riesling wines have been an important part of the winery's production and have had a most distinctive style. Dr Stewart makes his wines from fully ripened grapes, making them in a more full-bodied style than the majority of his neighbours. The largest part of the production is made in an off-dry style with just under 12° of alcohol and is sold simply as Columbia Valley Johannisberg Riesling. It has mouth-filling peachy fruit, quite crisp citrusy acidity, and is best drunk during the first three years of its life. The Stewart Vineyards Columbia Valley White Riesling is a shade lighter and noticeably sweeter, seeming slightly sweet-sour when it is tasted soon after release.

Since 1984 Stewart Vineyards has also produced a late-harvest Riesling every single vintage. The quality of these wines has varied quite markedly, but the best have been very fine. At their best thay have an intense bouquet of peaches, honey, and exotic fruits. Though no blockbusters, they have concentrated honeyed fruit on the palate, and a firm acidity that beautifully balances their high sweetness.

USSR

Total vineyard area (Ukraine): 993,000 acres

Vineyard area planted with Riesling (Ukraine): 1%/62,000 acres

Average annual Riesling production (Ukraine): 200,000,000 bottles

There is some viticulture in eleven of the fifteen Soviet republics, and significant table-wine production in four: Russia itself, Georgia, Moldavia, and the Ukraine. The latter is by far the most important wine producer, with 30 per cent of the Soviet Union's 3,300,000 acres of vineyards (second only to Spain). It is also in the Ukraine that by far the largest acreage of Riesling in the Soviet Union is to be found – indeed the Ukraine has the most extensive Riesling vineyards of any nation in the world.

Almost all the Soviet Union's vineyards for wine production are planted in a belt running round the northern coast of the Black Sea. The climate in the Ukraine is continental, with variations between mean winter and summer temperatures of as much as 50°C. Close to the Black Sea coast the winters are less bitingly cold, and the temperature variations are reduced owing to the moderating influence of the sea. Rainfall is low, and irrigation is necessary in many areas to make viticulture poss-ible. On the plus side, the region receives an enormous amount of sunshine, and with good vineyard management the grapes of even the latest-ripening noble European vine varieties can be fully ripened.

While Soviet viticulture has advanced considerably during the last decades, perhaps because of the challenge of the climatic extremes in its wine-growing regions, the wine-making technology in most of its wineries is rather primitive. Nevertheless, the Ukraine Riesling wines which I have been able to taste have been by no means bad. Though lacking freshness, they had some Riesling character in the bouquet, and, contrary to the image of Russian wine as being sticky sweet, they were well-balanced off-dry wines. The best were from the Crimea, which has the most temperate climate of the wine-growing areas in the Ukraine.

GLOSSARY

AUSLESE

Rich German and Austrian wines made from selectively harvested over-ripe/**botrytis**-affected grapes. Usually quite sweet, Auslese wines are intensely flavoured and long-lived. If the word **Trocken** also appears on the label the wine is full-bodied and dry.

BEERENAUSLESE
(BA)

Lusciously sweet German and Austrian wines made from shrivelled **botrytis**-affected grapes. Deep in colour, with honeyed aromas and flavours, Beerenauslese wines can only be produced in excellent vintages in very small quantities.

BOTRYTIS

When the *Botrytis cinerea* fungus affects ripe grapes, noble rot (*Edelfäule* in Germany, *pourriture noble* in France) results, and the grapes give a naturally sweet dessert wine.

CHAPTALIZATION

The addition of sugar to fermenting wine to increase its alcoholic content. This does not mean that the resulting wine will be any sweeter than if it had not been chaptalized.

CHARTA

An association of Rheingau wine-growers specializing in the production of high-quality dry wines. Strict selection system guarantees purity and quality. Charta

wines are promoted as an ideal complement to fine dining.

EISWEIN, *see* ICE WINE

HALBTROCKEN

German and Austrian designation for
off-dry wines. In Germany a Halbtrocken
wine may contain between 9 and 18 grams
unfermented sweetness per litre. In
Austria a Halbtrocken wine may contain
between 4 and 9 grams unfermented
sugar per litre.

ICE WINE

Produced from naturally frozen grapes,
ice wine is an extremely piquant style of
dessert wine which can be produced more
regularly than **BA** or **TBA**. Many North
American and Australasian wine-growers
take the short cut and use a freezer, rather
than wait for frost.

KABINETT

German Kabinett wines are the lightest
fine white wines in the world, typically
containing between 7.5° and 10° alcohol
(depending on the region and the vintage). They are usually off-dry with a racy
acidity. Austrian Kabinett wines are
invariably medium-bodied and dry.

MALOLACTIC
FERMENTATION

All red wines and many white wines
undergo malolactic fermentation as well
as alcoholic fermentation. Malolactic bac-
teria convert the unripe malic acid into
softer lactic acid. Few Riesling wines
undergo malolactic fermentation.

NOBLE ROT, *see* BOTRYTIS

ÖCHSLE

In the German-speaking world, the sugar content of grapes is measured in degrees Öchsle. The German and Austrian wine laws define wine quality by the Öchsle degree the grapes achieved.

QUALITÄTSWEIN (QBA)

A shortened form of *Qualitätswein bestimmter Anbaugebiete*, this is a German and Austrian designation for chaptalized wines. May be dry (**Trocken**), medium-dry (**Halbtrocken**), or lightly sweet in style. Often of ordinary quality, but not necessarily inferior.

SÉLECTION DES GRAINS NOBLES (SGN)

Designation for rich dessert wines made in Alsace from shrivelled **botrytis**-affected grapes. With similar honeyed flavours to German or Austrian **BAs**, Alsace SGNs are usually more alcoholic.

SPÄTLESE

German and Austrian designation for medium-bodied wines made from late-harvested grapes. Usually off-dry or lightly sweet with more depth and elegance than **QbA** or **Kabinett** wines, they can also be vinified dry, in which case **Trocken** appears on the label.

TROCKEN

German and Austrian designation for dry wines. In Germany (excepting Franken) Trocken wines can contain up to 9 grams unfermented sweetness per litre. In Franken and Austria, Trocken wines can contain up to 4 grams unfermented sugar per litre.

TROCKENBEEREN-AUSLESE (TBA)

Intensely sweet and extremely concentrated German and Austrian wines made from raisined **botrytis**-affected grapes. Similar in style to **Beerenauslese** yet even more unctuous, Trockenbeerenauslese is rarely produced more than once a decade.

VENDANGE
TARDIVE (VT)

French designation for late-harvested wines made in Alsace. Always rich and powerful, Vendange Tardive wines are sometimes vinified dry, and are sometimes slightly sweet.

VIN DE GLACE, *see* ICE WINE

INDEX

ATLANTIC

OCEAN

Equator

PACIFIC

OCEAN